Why I am a Christian

Why I am a Christian

Kent Philpott

EVANGELICAL PRESS

EVANGELICAL PRESS
Faverdale North Industrial Estate, Darlington, DL3 0PH,
England

Evangelical Press USA
P. O. Box 84, Auburn, MA 01501, USA

e-mail: sales@evangelicalpress.org

web: http://www.evangelicalpress.org

First published 2002

British Library Cataloguing in Publication Data available

ISBN 0 85234 501 1

Printed and bound in Great Britain by Creative Print and
Design Wales, Ebbw Vale, South Wales.

Contents

1.
Why I am a Christian

1.
Why I am a Christian

Given all the barriers and obstacles that stood in my way I am surprised I became a Christian at all. There were so many hindrances that, thinking of them now, I am amazed afresh that I was ever converted. It could have gone either way, too. Immediately prior to my conversion I thought that I might walk away without Christ for ever.

After thirty-seven years as a Christian and thirty-four years as a minister of the gospel, I have discovered a number of obstacles, hindrances, barriers, or scandals that may keep a person from becoming a Christian. What these obstacles are and how they may be overcome is the subject of this chapter. To put it another way: 'Why am I a Christian?'

The exclusiveness of Jesus

The idea of Jesus being the only Saviour was, to my mind, an expression of ignorance and arrogance. To many non-believers, the idea that Jesus is God seems absurd. To their thinking, the claim that Jesus is the exclusive means to the creator of the entire universe appears puerile and simplistic.

At the time of my conversion my concept of God was confused. I had a notion that there might be a God, but to admit that there is a particular God who had become a man and had acted to bring a rebellious people to himself was beyond the scope of my understanding. And to suggest that this God was the only true God offended the liberal sensitivities I had gained through the course of my college education.

Some liberal Christians, and others of course, have abandoned the concept of the exclusiveness of Jesus. Inclusiveness, diversity, political correctness, relativism — these are powerful ideas and have persuaded many to deny the exclusive claims of the Bible about Christ. This departure from historic Christian doctrine may be enough for some to reject the claims of Christianity. But many Christians still adhere to Scripture, and thus, the barrier stands. If, at the time of my pre-conversion crisis, I had encountered someone championing the cause of liberal Christianity I may well have been persuaded by his reasoning, or at least would have become more confused than I already was. Instead, I heard a preacher who stuck to the Book and would not compromise one inch.

Still, the notion that God should only 'love' Christians violates a certain sense of fairness. What about those in Africa, and elsewhere, who did not know anything about Jesus? What about *them*? What kind of a God is this, anyway? What about those who could not find their way to the narrow path: would they be condemned for ever in a devil's hell? Particularly

heartbreaking to many is the idea that the innocents of
the world, the children, and those raised in deplorable
and hopeless conditions and who, more than likely,
would never even hear of Jesus, will be lost for ever.
For me, this is perhaps the most troubling of all aspects
even though I am in my fourth decade as a Christian. It
will probably trouble me all my life. There are no words
I can think of to settle my mind about it. Yet I know the
God and Father of my Lord Jesus Christ is loving and
merciful beyond description. There is abundant testimony in the Bible that God loves everyone. This I am
sure of. Therefore I will leave the hard questions for
him to answer in his way and in his time. Even such
tough questions as these do not have the power to dis-
tort or negate the truth of Jesus and his cross.

This particular barrier did not come down by logic
or revelation; I figured nothing out at all. Now, all these
years later, I can reconcile the difficulty of the exclusiveness of Jesus more easily, though not completely.
However, it has occurred to me that a creator God, sin-
gle of purpose and plan as I thought reasonable for a
God to be, might well respond in the same way to all
his creation. Why have a host of different plans? It would
only serve to confuse everyone. A God who changed
constantly would not be much of a God. A God who
treated people differently may well be a confused God.
Furthermore, why would the Creator send his own Son,
in fact come himself (here we encounter the mysterious
but essential doctrine of the Trinity), and be brutalized
by his very own chosen people, if it meant so little?

It should also be pointed out that the gods of the
world's religions are quite different from one another.

This is not a treatise on world religions, but the plain fact is, they are not the same despite the sophistry of the masses, which claims, 'All paths lead to the same God.' I have read the basics of the world's religions and their belief systems exclude one another; this is especially true for Hinduism/Buddhism and Christianity. Using a popular means of comparing things: it is not apples and apples. It is more like apples and kumquats, and even this comparison does not highlight the tremendous differences.

There is no question but that the 'Jesus only' barrier is enough to keep someone from Christ. It nearly kept me from him.

Judgement and hell

Most non-believers know that Christians claim their God knows all things and is all powerful. Why would such a God create people who have personal flaws, which make them likely to break his laws, and then predestine them to spend eternity in hell? Such a God seems monstrously capricious and cruel.

What troubled me was the question, 'How could a loving God condemn one of his creatures to a horrible place for ever?' This was the nature of the barrier.

The preacher presented it loud and clear — judgement and hell awaited all who did not trust in Jesus. It was here that a 'fire and brimstone' Baptist preacher confronted me. The liberal preachers, heavy on love and soft on wrath, did not convince me, though I am not sure why not. I suppose I already believed what they taught:

to be sincere and loving, sit in church and pray, give to those less fortunate and do good works — that was their whole message. But in the back of my mind I wondered. If these universal salvation preachers were right then I had nothing to worry about. If they were wrong, I was in trouble. Not that I was a terribly awful person, but I definitely was not holy and without sin. And I had no plan to change. I thought that the few sins I committed to supposedly help me to cope with the troubles of life were innocent enough. There were just a few major ones from my youth, and I thought I could work on them somehow.

Yet the thundering from the pulpit made God sound awful to me. I thought it would have been wiser to delete those points on judgement and hell and be, in today's jargon, a more 'user friendly' church. I wondered if the preacher knew what he was doing. This was not good psychology. But he persisted in it. To be fair though, to be accurate really, he did not mention it much, maybe once or twice; but I could not get it out of my mind.

I would not be frightened into becoming a Christian, nor would I change my ways. If I had to go to hell, I thought, I would not be alone. If that was my due, then so be it. So getting me all worked up about hell would not do the trick.

Would Jesus really say to human beings, 'Depart from me, I never knew you'? The preacher said he would. Would the torment be so terrible that a condemned person would plead for even a drop of water? And would it mean being shut up for ever with the demons and the devil? The preacher said it would, because that is what the Bible taught.

I never did resolve the problem of judgement and hell before my conversion, and it still is quite a problem to me. I believe those doctrines because I see them throughout the Scriptures, and they are entirely logical. They even make sense to me. God made a perfect world, created humans in his own image, who then rebelled against him and thus lost the fellowship they had with him. Their sin separated, or, more precisely, severed the relationship between them and their God. Now death would mean that humans could not be with God where he dwells, in heaven.

They cannot be in his holy presence with their sin against them. And because they would be raised to everlasting life they had to spend it elsewhere — in a place called hell. This hell, created as an everlasting abode for the devil and demons, would be the final home of the unrighteous. This is the sentence to be handed down at the final judgement of God.

There it is: judgement and hell. What a barrier! We, with our limited understanding, are offended by such an idea. It is an obstacle so high that no one can get over it on his own.

The problem of grace

How can grace be a problem? Grace — the love, mercy and forgiveness of God given freely to those who do not deserve them — is indeed a wonderful gift.

Grace is God electing us to salvation. Since we cannot come to him on our own, he comes to us. We have no ability to come to him. Rather, the Father draws us to his Son. And when he does, we hear the voice of Jesus calling out to us, we hear him knocking, and we arise and open that door. He comes in and dwells with us because it is his will and desire to do so.

But grace is a barrier because it implies that we cannot control our own destiny. This is the heart of it. Inasmuch as grace is a gift from God, it follows that we are powerless to make ourselves acceptable to God. We cannot forgive our own sin; no matter what we do, we cannot make ourselves righteous.

In my self-righteousness and pride I proclaimed: 'I am a good person, as good or better than anyone else, and what's more, I am a spiritual and compassionate person.' The biblical doctrine of grace denotes that all of these fine qualities are of no value whatsoever when it comes to being right before God. And it made me angry.

The Scriptures declare: 'It does not, therefore, depend upon man's desire or effort, but on God's mercy' (Romans 9:16). Since grace is offensive to us, we are tempted to invent a religion by which we can earn our own way. This is the foundation of all religions except biblical Christianity. The opposite of grace expresses itself like this: earn my own way, do it myself, work hard, study hard, be sincere, love others, serve those in need, attain to a loving and compassionate consciousness, and so on. But in our pride we reject grace, for grace is really God giving to us what we cannot earn. We stubbornly refuse grace and say, 'Away with it, I will do it myself. I am man, I am woman, I am my own person.' We proudly proclaim, 'I am even my own god.' Tell me I am in control, the master of my fate, and I will bow down and worship before this altar and this god created in my image. Declare that I am without sin or already forgiven or that there is no such thing as sin and I will embrace such ideas enthusiastically. But don't tell me I am a sinner, dead and lost and condemned, or I might rise up and in a rare moment of intolerance accuse you of being narrow and bigoted, or worse.

The self-willed person cannot extinguish the offensive nature of grace. This barrier will not be removed, for if grace is removed there can be no forgiveness. Jesus has done all that is necessary, all that can ever be done for my salvation. Now he stands offering it to me freely. This is grace. When I did not love him, he loved me. When I despised and rejected him, he longed to be my Saviour. When I heaped abuse upon him, he prayed that I might be forgiven. This is grace.

Grace challenges most of my life experience because I have been taught to expect punishment or rewards depending on my behaviour. But grace contradicts this universal experience. Outside of the grace of Jesus we know only karma, reward or punishment, and the best we can hope for is an even break. But we cannot break even, in reality we will only experience repeated failure, guilt and despair.

What a barrier — without Jesus we can do nothing. Yet when we see this great and liberating truth, we can experience grace and the obstacle will be overcome.

The devil and the demons

What proof is there of a devil? There is none that would stand up to scientific scrutiny, even though those who are committed to the reality of paranormal experiences may advance certain evidence.

The world's religions are full of stories of demons and devils, most may be fanciful and mythical, but the fact remains that the people on earth believe and have believed in the demonic from the beginning. There are probably more religious ceremonies, litanies and rituals designed to ward off evil spirits, or at least to placate them, than any other religious activity taking place on a day by day basis. But this alone proves nothing.

The Bible speaks of a literal devil, named Satan. It also speaks of demons. In short, Satan was a ruling angel who rebelled against God at some time in the distant past, and the demons are those angels who sided with him in that rebellion. These beings then allied themselves against the one supreme deity and all that this Creator God made — especially that which was created in his own image, humans. Yet, this 'proof' does not measure up to scientific examination either. The existence of Satan and demons is a matter of faith. Though some claim direct experience with the devil, as I do myself, yet it is subjective in nature and not the kind of proof that would stand up to scientific inquiry.

Counter arguments for the devil's existence, though compelling, prove nothing either. For the sake of fairness, I will point out some of the more potent arguments against the reality of demonic forces. Firstly, if God knows everything, then why didn't he know that some of his angels would rebel and therefore refrain from creating the rebellious ones? Secondly, if God has complete power to do anything, then why didn't he destroy the rebellious angels before they could harm people?

Thirdly, if Satan and the demons will be cast into hell some time in the future, then why doesn't God do away with them right now? Fourthly, if God created soon-to-be-fallen angels, then why didn't he make them interested in tadpoles, so that people would be left in peace? Fifthly, if God created angels who would fall, they why doesn't he admit his mistake? Sixthly, if it is not a mistake, then God must not love his people all that much.

A thorough examination of the Bible would satisfy us on some of these points, but even armed with scriptural explanations, the existence of the demonic would still be a matter of faith. Furthermore, several of the counter arguments bring up the issue of theodicy, or the justification of a good God in the face of evil, a subject long and futilely debated over the millenniums.

So, then, we have the problem of how preposterous the existence of the devil may seem. And if, in fact, there is a devil, then that should lead us also to wonder what influence such a crafty, subtle and powerful being (as the Bible depicts Satan) has upon us. Prior to my conversion, had I been blinded or somehow influenced by the devil? I don't know whether I had been or not. If in fact I had, I was unaware of it.

Sometimes I ask myself where all my antagonism against Christianity, the Bible, church and Christians came from. Did it all belong to me alone? I think it is possible, but based on what I know now, I think the devil must bear at least some of the responsibility.

Indeed the devil's existence still seems preposterous to me. I haven't figured out why evil exists or why a loving God would allow evil to exist in the first place. I doubt I ever will. Now I have some idea of the resolution of these issues tucked away in a systematic theological model in the back of my mind, but it is virtually impossible for me to recapitulate it to anyone. If pressed, I would say that Jesus believed in the existence of both Satan and demons. This is the most telling point for me inasmuch as Jesus has ultimate integrity for me. He is Truth himself and I have learned I can trust him.

Regarding the other point, given the reality of the demonic: How might the demonic influence a human being? Paul wrote, 'The god of this age has blinded the minds of unbelievers, so that they cannot see the light of the gospel of the glory of Christ, who is the image of God' (2 Corinthians 4:4). Satan, the god of this age, blinds minds so that people either cannot perceive Jesus at all or fail to understand his message. Usually it is the latter.

In my case I did not understand that Jesus was the Son of God, the Saviour. That he was a historical figure who actually lived on earth was not a problem for me. I believed Jesus was a founder of a religion and considered him to be a great teacher, but I never believed he was the Saviour who took my sin upon himself on the cross and who later rose from the dead.

When Jesus died upon the cross, he won the great victory over the devil. In fact, Jesus completely defeated Satan and will finally put Satan away for ever into hell when he returns at the end of the age. Although Satan has power to blind the minds of non-believers, he does not have ultimate power. The Father calls people to his Son Jesus according to his own will. The apostle John put it this way: 'The reason the Son of God appeared was to destroy the devil's work' (1 John 3:8).

Perhaps the most vivid example of Jesus' triumph over Satan is the story of the man dwelling in the tombs in a region known as the Gerasenes. He had a legion, that is, many, many, demons living in him. This outcast had been reduced to the most horrible existence and was beyond the help of anyone, but when he met Jesus the demons that had tormented and demented him were cast into a herd of pigs. Now in his right mind, he became an evangelist to his countrymen (see Luke 8:26-39). This is perfectly in tune with what Jesus said he would do. 'The thief comes only to steal and kill and destroy; I have come that they may have life, and have it to the full' (John 10:10).

'Blessed is the one who takes no offence at me.' These words of Jesus are the reason for this book. Piled up four deep now, the hindrances might seem insurmountable, but they are nothing but straw. There is no real offence in Jesus.

The scandalous history of the church

There are two churches today and it has been like this from the beginning. One church is visible, the organization, the institution, and it is far from perfect, sometimes very far from anything resembling perfect. The other is the true church, probably tiny in proportion to the visible church, and is made up of all those who are genuine, born-again Christians. This true church may be intermingled with the institutional church while parts of the true church may exist outside of it altogether.

'For the message of the cross is foolishness to those who are perishing, but to us who are being saved it is the power of God' (1 Corinthians 1:18). Because of this truth, there has been an effort on the part of church leaders, almost right from the beginning and throughout the course of church history, to avoid the scandal of the cross. Since the cross is foolishness to so many, there is a desire to replace it with ideas more readily acceptable to worldly people. It might be said that the true church consists of those who are born again of the Spirit and adhere to and preach the message of the cross where Jesus, God in the flesh, died for our sin. This church cannot be identified with any one group, denomination, theological model, or leader.

The visible church, churches really, with all the various names, doctrines and leaders, developed political power, accumulated wealth, and worst of all, devised magical means whereby forgiveness and salvation were dispensed, and came to represent what all the world thought was biblical Christianity — but was not.

Therefore there are two histories of the church, and most of us are not able to easily distinguish between them. In his book *Concerning Scandals*, John Calvin wrote that the church 'never shines with that splendour, which would enable the minds of men to recognize the Kingdom of God'.

Even the true church, the church that clings to the cross of Jesus, is itself not pure and free from error because it is composed of sinners darkened in their understanding. It is no surprise that the church and everything associated with it is prone to scandal.

The history of the early church, as found in the New Testament book of Acts, reveals a less than perfect collection of believers. Acts 5 records members of the church lying to the apostles about money. Acts 6 contains details of trouble over the unequal distribution of food to certain widows, when the apostles themselves were implicated. In Acts 15 there is the account of a debate about the doctrine of salvation. Of the seven churches in Asia (see the opening chapters of Revelation) only one church escaped Jesus' criticism altogether. There is more, but the point is that the church is not pictured as absolutely perfect in its most important and public document, the Bible. The early church had its problems, and Paul, in particular, wrote several letters to correct various congregations. Curiously, the church's internal difficulties escaped any would-be censors. The Bible records it all because that is what happened.

It should be understood then that what history might call the church was (and is) not necessarily the church at all, but only a worldly institution that has some true believers. We think of the crusades, the witch trials of Salem, the Inquisition, forced conversions of Jews and a thousand other atrocities — can this all be laid at the door of the church? The institutional church, or some form of it, is responsible for these and other horrible events. But so much of the scandal, probably most of it, cannot legitimately be laid at the door of the elect church of God. How much we will never know. Since we are all sinners, while still saints, there will be one grievous episode after the other, but I believe there is less true scandal than most people might imagine.

One reason the church's history is full of such scandal is that the enemy of God, Satan, and those who belong to that dark kingdom, fight a dirty and terrible war against all those who trust in Jesus. Consider the following. Jesus warned that false Christs and prophets would appear and perform great signs and wonders so that even the true Christians might be deceived (see Matthew 24:24). Paul wrote something similar: 'The Spirit clearly says that in later times some will abandon the faith and follow deceiving spirits and things taught by demons' (1 Timothy 4:1). In addition, Paul warned the Corinthian church about false teachers operating in the midst of the church itself: 'For such men are false apostles, deceitful workmen, masquerading as apostles of Christ' (2 Corinthians 11:13). In the organized church there will be false apostles empowered by Satan himself. Is it any wonder then that the history of such a church is full of scandal?

Remember, the good and bad elements of the church are so intermingled that it is often impossible to tell the difference. In a parable, Jesus warned against trying to make distinctions. His warning is so pertinent to a proper understanding of the mixed nature of the church it is quoted here at length.

'The kingdom of heaven is like a man who sowed good seed in his field. But while everyone was sleeping, his enemy came and sowed weeds among the wheat, and went away. When the wheat sprouted and formed heads, then the weeds also appeared.

'The owner's servants came to him and said, "Sir, didn't you sow good seed in your field? Where then did the weeds come from?"

'"An enemy did this," he replied.

'The servants asked him, "Do you want us to go and pull them up?"

'"No," he answered, "because while you are pulling the weeds, you may root up the wheat with them. Let both grow together until the harvest. At that time I will tell the harvesters: First collect the weeds and tie them in bundles to be burned; then gather the wheat and bring it into my barn"'

(Matthew 13:24-30).

Like any diabolic and clever opponent, Satan's tactic is to attack the message by attacking the messenger. In the broadest sense, the church is that messenger and so must be besmirched by the archenemy. This must be understood in order to have an accurate understanding of church history.

There is a true church, the church elect and called by God; and he alone knows who are his. This church is perfect because it is the Body of Christ. And Christ is in the midst of his church, the Church Triumphant. This church is gathered to worship, honour and serve the God and Father of our Lord Jesus Christ. To this church Jesus promised that the gates of hell would not prevail against it. The history of the church demonstrates the truth of Jesus' statement despite the fact that from those hellish gates every foul and scandalous evil will emerge.

The hypocrisy of believers

All Christians are hypocrites and because of this, non-believers will be tempted to reject Jesus.

Webster's New Universal Unabridged Dictionary defines 'hypocrite' as 'a person who pretends to have virtues, moral and religious, beliefs, principles, etc., that he or she does not actually possess, especially a person whose actions belie stated beliefs' (1996 edition). I have to admit to falling into the category of a hypocrite on the basis of this definition.

Prior to my conversion I knew that Christians were hypocrites; in fact, I used it as an excuse to reject Christian claims. One girl who I heard was a Christian and I knew attended church was notoriously promiscuous. Some of my friends dated her and it made me particularly angry that she would not go out with me. Whether she was a real Christian I could not say, but the whole situation served to prejudice me against Christianity.

My perception, although I am not sure where it came from, was that Christians had to be perfect. Okay, so you are a Christian, I reasoned, so then you have to be perfectly loving and ethical. And if not, then, 'Ah ha, see! You are a fake and a liar and your Christianity is bogus, too.' This is how I saw things and it suited my rebellion perfectly.

There is no question but that I am a hypocrite, too. It is not my intention to be one, but I find that I am. A hypocrite is someone who professes to be one thing and is not. I profess to be perfect in Christ, but I am far less than that. There is a sense, however, in which I am perfect, because God considers me as perfect since I had been placed into Christ at the moment of my conversion. But I am still a sinner, not perfect, and I will remain so until the very moment of my death.

Christians will do the strangest things, as I know from my experience as a pastor for several decades. Even the best of us fall short of the ideal because the standard is so very high — Jesus himself. When his life is examined it is clear that he was no hypocrite. No, he is the Lamb of God without blemish; though tempted to sin in every way that we are, he is without sin of any kind. This sinless one said that we are to be perfect as the Father in heaven is perfect, and therein lies the problem.

The 'perfect yet sinner' paradox is true of all Christians, and it is quite biblical. Paul confessed that the things he did not want to do he did, and conversely, the things he wanted to do, he did not do (Romans 7:15-20). And what a scandal this has all produced. If anyone is looking for a reason to castigate Christianity, he will not have far to look. I should point out that a careful examination of Paul's life would not have revealed him to be some kind of wild sinner indulging the flesh at every opportunity. In fact, it might have taken a close examination to find anything amiss at all. But Paul knew the high calling he had in Christ and, when being honest with himself, he would have had to admit that he did not always act in accordance with his calling.

In the pages of the New Testament there are stories of some notable hypocrites. Peter comes immediately to mind. He was the first of the apostles to confess that Jesus was the Messiah. Then, before very long, he denied Jesus three times. There were also the two zealous disciples in the early Jerusalem church, Ananias and his wife Sapphira, who turned out to be cheats and liars (Acts 5:1-5). One of Paul's companions, a missionary by the name of Demas, completely abandoned Paul, the gospel, and Christ, rebelled, and returned to a sinful life (see 2 Timothy 4:9-10). Consider, however, that the biblical writers made no attempt to hide or clean up the historical record. They let it stand as it was. Hypocrisy was expected because the integrity and truth of Christianity does not reside with individual Christians, but depends exclusively on Jesus alone who is the solid foundation and ground of it all.

Christians are bound to appear as hypocrites. We have always known this. Some of the greatest heroes in the history of the post-apostolic church have been inconsistent, although 'inconsistent' is far too innocuous a term to describe some of the antics of the saints. Acknowledging this in *Concerning Scandals*, John Calvin wrote, 'It is wrong for us to measure the eternal truth of God by the changing inconstancy of men' (p. 78). Then in the same place, he continued, 'Will the treacherous desertion of certain individuals overthrow our faith?' Of course he expects the answer to be a resounding 'No!'

Early in my Christian life I could not help but notice that I did not give up sinning even though I wanted to. At one point I thought I should not be spending any time with those 'good people' down at the church. It was not enough that no one knew what a rascal I was; I knew it and so I thought that Christianity must not be working. Yet I hung on, refused to give up, and finally realized that everyone was just the same as me.

As time went on I believed I was making a little progress. I noticed that although some of my sin seemed to stop, but that I would develop, or rather discover, new sins. This has been the case the entire time I have been a Christian. I am never going to get away from the fact that I am a hypocrite. Hopefully non-believers will not use my failures and inconsistencies to reject the gospel. I have decided that I do not want to hide from people in order to keep my sin private. No, I want to live an honest and open life. So, I intend to grow up into the stature of the fulness of Christ and even when anyone gets to know me very well, they will not be caused to stumble by what they see.

Christians are bound to be seen as hypocrites by those who want to rebel against God. All they have to do is watch one of us for a while and they will soon find some indiscretion, real or imagined, and that will be enough to turn them from Christ. This barrier can only be over-come by the Holy Spirit of God working to convert a sinner.

The trouble with the Bible

How I despised the Bible! One day I caught my wife reading it and in anger I took it from her hands, threw it across the room, and ordered her never to bring a Bible into our apartment again.

Later, I had to read portions of the Bible for a term paper for a college philosophy of religion course. Failing to understand anything about it I became so frustrated that I vowed never to touch a Bible again.

This is the trouble with the Bible — it is incomprehensible to those who do not have the Spirit of God.

Paul put it this way: 'The man without the Spirit does not accept the things that come from the Spirit of God, for they are foolishness to him, and he cannot understand them, because they are spiritually discerned' (1 Corinthians 2:14). I can personally verify the truth of this verse, and in addition, I have observed this in hundreds of people over the years. Many people who had consistently avoided the Bible developed a thirst for it after their conversion, which never went away.

In our unconverted state we rebel against the Bible and what it teaches. This rebellion may take a passive or aggressive form. My own was aggressive, illustrated by my throwing a Bible across the room. Most people's rebellion takes a passive form — they simply ignore it. Even many well-educated people do this despite the fact that the Bible is the most influential book ever published in our culture. Whether one agrees with it or not, more copies of it are printed each year than any other book. The Bible, with its wonderful and timeless stories, flowing language and flawless grammar, transcending all other books, is being ignored by the literati.

Why is this so? The reason has already been expressed — the Bible is a spiritual book and unless the Spirit of God reveals its truth it will remain unintelligible. Furthermore, the Bible does not flatter the human spirit. The Bible calls sin sin, and it does so in no uncertain terms. It also presents a God to whom every person is responsible since he will judge the living and the dead according to their faith in his Son, Jesus Christ. The Bible is rejected because of its message. We react against the Bible because we have broken God's laws and have become corrupt.

One of the difficulties with the Bible is that it is written by real people, and their personalities and peculiar literary styles are apparent. Therefore it does not appear to be a spiritual book at all. The Bible is the history of God, or stories about God and his people, from the creation to the prophecies about the end of the universe, told by flawed and imperfect people, although under the inspiration of the Holy Spirit. The ancient people of God pieced it together over a very long period of time. It is unlike any other religious or spiritual document in existence.

I cannot prove that the Bible is the true word of God. Certainly I could, if there was space, make a strong case for it. There is plenty of solid evidence that points towards that conclusion. I could speak at length of prophecies fulfilled; or of forty authors over a 1500-year span, in three languages and even more cultures, from Moses to John of the Revelation, weaving the same, seamless cloth; or of countless numbers of people over the course of thousands of years whose lives have been redeemed, transformed and rescued through the Book's direct influence; or of the great nations and institutions whose foundation is the great Book; but none of it would be enough to prove the inspiration of the Bible objectively. It is a matter of faith, it is subjective, and when proven in this way, that proof is stronger than anything objective could ever be.

For me, the one great proof for the authenticity of the Bible is that Jesus believed the Old Testament to be the very word of God. Moreover, the New Testament is the record of Jesus, his life and ministry. Therefore Jesus is the reason for my confidence in it all.

I trust Jesus. It is that simple. Having examined his life, by reading the Gospels a hundred times or more, I find Jesus to be the very definition of integrity. In him there is no inconsistency, no pride or selfishness, no hint of sin, vainglory or deceit. In all his ways and words, he is pure and holy. No one has ever been able to prove against him any wrongdoing. So I trust the Scriptures because I trust Jesus.

Even this argument, however, will not persuade the sceptic. The Bible will always be troublesome until the Author reveals himself to the reader.

The last great obstacle — sin

It is all about sin. Sinning begins with the breaking of a known law of God. Perhaps it is lying. At first it is easy to lie, but once the barrier is broken, it is easier the next time and the next and the next. What was once so unnatural becomes natural and easy. Peter said a man is a slave to whatever has mastered him (2 Peter 2:19). Sin becomes a habit at some point, usually sooner rather than later, and after that an obsession. Beyond that, sinning becomes addictive. We sin more and more until finally we *have* to. Even when dire consequences become apparent, we cannot stop ourselves. We will sin for the pleasure even if it is only for a moment. Indeed some people are so mired in sin, depend so heavily upon some sin or another, that they are seemingly hopelessly addicted. The thought of giving it up is so frightening that they will do almost anything to hold on to it. People will ruin their lives in order to avoid repentance. But worse — they will subject themselves to eternal ruin.

Sin is more often embraced than repented of. Indeed, sinful behaviour will more quickly be tolerated, if not applauded, than abhorred. Yes, sin will even be championed, defended and promoted in an effort to take the sting out of the conscience. This process is sometimes called 'liberation'. Within a classical definition of the word 'liberal' is the notion of breaking free from the law of God. And the question comes: 'Breaking free to do what?' The answer is simple enough: 'Sin'.

We all have sinned and fallen short of the glory of God. We know it, too, and that is why the word 'sin' is hated above all others. Mention the word in the wrong company and a riot could ensue. Talk about sin and hearts are hardened, teeth are set on edge, consciences are stirred, passions are enflamed and minds are closed. Even if the word is not defined with biblical accuracy, it will still get a reaction.

Preachers have been beaten, killed even, for mentioning the word in a sermon. Holy Hubert, who was famous in the Jesus Movement and routinely preached on the steps of Sproul Hall at the University of California's Berkeley campus, had all his front teeth knocked out, one by one, for telling the hippies they were 'dirty rotten sinners'. I know, because I acted as his unofficial bodyguard on more than one occasion. How those mellow pacifists became enraged over the word 'sin'!

Before my conversion it irritated me to hear the preacher say that because I had not trusted in Christ to save me, I was a sinner. He said I had to turn from my sin, and he made it sound as if everything I did was sinful.

I did not consider myself a sinner at all; 'no worse than the average guy' was my motto. But as the months

went by, although I do not know how, I became convinced I actually was a sinner. It is only with the
advantage of hindsight that I can say that it was the
work of the Holy Spirit. In any case, the truth became
clear to me — I stood guilty before God.

At first I tried to clean up, do better, stop that and
start this — the usual effort by a sinner who does not
want to turn to Christ. I would put an end to one sin
but discover two more or even start up a new one.

Sin and wickedness are related. In the dark recesses
of our soul, sin is enshrined. But when the light of Jesus
is cast on it, then the sin is seen for the utter corruption
that it is. And this realization makes us most uncomfortable. I squirmed and wriggled, rationalized and
compromised, but it was to no avail. Unable to find a
way out on my own, my eyes were turned to Jesus, and
I knew he was my only hope. Once I saw that Jesus was
the Saviour, I could not be kept from him. And this is
usually how it is; Jesus becomes irresistible.

Sin is mysterious and powerful, blinding and ad-
dicting, a deadly spiritual cancer. Sin is so overwhelming that no one can overcome it. Only God can forgive,
cleanse and restore us. And this great work took place
on the cross where Jesus shed his blood and died in our
place, taking the believer's sin upon himself and suffering the consequences. His resurrection is proof that
our sin can be forgiven.

Before my conversion to Christ, my friends and I
enjoyed the 'fellowship of sin'. We reinforced each
other's sinful ways, approved of our mutual transgres-
sions, sneered at the goodie-two-shoes and righteous
Christians who weren't having any fun, and tried to

convince ourselves that we were 'cool guys' who really knew how to enjoy life. Once I came to Christ, I lost these friends who wanted to continue in this fellowship of sin. At the time I was hurt; I did not see that God was doing me a favour. The sinful fellowship was replaced by a better one, and it was God's plan because I would never have been able to break free on my own.

The obstacle of sin is overcome by the inward working of the Holy Spirit. This holy and interior working of God helps us to repent, even gives us a hungering and thirsting after righteousness. Paul expressed it in these words: 'For it is God who works in you to will and to act according to his good purpose' (Philippians 2:13). It will come to pass that we will gladly let sin go that we might have Jesus and his righteousness.

The real reason why I am a Christian

God himself removed the obstacles and overcame the problems. A young man, probably not unlike myself, asked Jesus, 'What good thing must I do to get eternal life?' (Matthew 19:16). Jesus essentially told the man that he could not do it on his own. Jesus' disciples overheard the conversation and were greatly astonished. They asked, 'Who then can be saved?' (v. 25).

Jesus answered, 'With man this is impossible, but with God all things are possible' (v. 26).

Left to myself I only had obstacle piled on top of obstacle. I could not repent; I could not believe. But I wanted to because I knew I must. In a moment, though, the obstacles were brushed aside. It was as though Jesus called me personally to himself. I wanted him. My lost condition threatened to destroy me for ever but I knew Jesus was the Saviour. This truth, now clear to me, would not let me go.

Jesus seemed to stand before me calling out my name. The Saviour who had borne my sin when hanging on a cross, the one who had shed his own blood to cleanse me of my sin, the one who had died and had been buried, the one who had risen from the dead and is alive for evermore — this Jesus called me to himself, and in a way I do not fully understand. And it was done right there and then.

This is why I am a Christian.

2.
A death blow to Christianity?

2.
A death blow to Christianity?

The Mars Polar Landing

On 3 December 1999 NASA's Mars Polar Landing spacecraft blasted off in hopes of finding life on Mars. It appears now that the effort failed as the craft cannot be contacted — the costly vehicle is lost. The Mars Polar Landing project is but one of many attempts aimed at discovering life somewhere in the universe beyond earth. For instance, SETI (search for extraterrestrial intelligence) is a mammoth effort using radio telescopes to intercept radio and other electronic emissions from intelligent life maybe many hundreds of light years away. There is enormous interest in this, as the fascination with aliens and UFOs on the non-scientific level illustrates. NASA's effort is directed by some of the best minds in the scientific community and is one I follow closely.

Implications

In an interview in connection with the Mars Landing Probe, Mark Lupisella, a scientist at the NASA Astrobiology Institute in Greenbelt, Maryland, said that

the discovery of life outside the earth could have impli-
cations for the traditional religions — meaning Judaism
and Christianity presumably. In fact, he implied that
such a discovery would be a 'death blow' (my termin-
ology) to the traditional religions and that people would
no longer find them credible or need them.[1]

Mark Lupisella means that the discovery of life in
the universe other than on earth would mean that life
could spring up anywhere, where the conditions were
right, thus diminishing the need for a creator God if not
negating it altogether. And this seems to be the prevailing mood I encounter as I watch the scientific attempts to find life, intelligent or not, in the universe.
Such a discovery would apparently reinforce the extreme view of many Darwinists that evolutionary theory
accounts for the existence of life and that all the creation stories are therefore simply mythological.

What about extraterrestrial life?

Does the Bible say anything directly about the existence or non-existence of extraterrestrial life? I do not
think that it does.

Does the Bible, and/or doctrine derived from it,
imply or infer that there is or is not life elsewhere in the
universe? Again I do not think so, though I know there
will be differing opinions within the Christian community.

In the book of Genesis it is written that God the creator
made man 'in his own image ... male and female he
created them' (1:27). This creation took place on planet
earth and there is no record of life being created anywhere else. The Scriptures do not say explicitly that

God's work of creating life only occurred here but that is the picture one gets. Basing a belief, however, that life is only possible on earth, it may be conceded, is one rooted in silence. At any rate, believing one or the other is acceptable biblically — and I do not think that adhering to one or the other should warrant the application of either the conservative or liberal label.

For me, whether there is life elsewhere is irrelevant — certainly not a death blow to my faith. As a matter of interest, I do not think there is life created in the image of God anywhere else in the universe; but this is an extrabiblical concept of mine, not one I can prove from Scripture — it is pure speculation. Yes, I would be surprised if humans or other forms of intelligent life that had an accurate, I mean biblical, concept of God were to be discovered somewhere in the universe. I think it is possible, though, that life may be found, even life forms resembling mammals, or life forms structurally identical to human beings, somewhere other than the earth. Looking like a human being does not mean that such a creature is created in the image of God, for the image of God is spiritual, not physical. (The Neanderthal and Cro-Magnon fossils have not persuaded me that they are creatures made in the image of God.)

The reason for my conviction

The reason for my conviction that the existence of life forms in places other than our earth is ultimately irrelevant, albeit interesting, is the actual existence of the person and work of Jesus Christ. That God the Father sent his Son to this earth is uncontrovertible. If life forms anatomically similar to human beings were found on every planet and moon in the universe it would not change the reality of who Jesus is and what he did. And this is not a case of hiding my head in the proverbial sand or a refusal to face scientific fact. No, Jesus is the one unchangeable fact, the one truth that I measure all else by. Being the same yesterday, today, and for ever, he is the only constant in the chaotic, ever-changing universe where even scientific 'truth' comes and goes.

The case of Spurgeon

C. H. Spurgeon was a student of astronomy, an amateur certainly, but well versed in the science of his day. In his *Lectures To My Students*[2] is this somewhat lengthy but significant quote:

> The nearest planet that revolves around the sun is Mercury, which is about 37,000,000 miles from the great luminary. Mercury, therefore, receives a far greater allowance of light and heat from the sun than comes to us upon the earth. It is believed that, even at the poles of Mercury, water would always boil; that is to say, if the planet is constituted at all as this world is. None of us could possibly live there; but that is no reason why other people should not, for God could make some of his creatures to live in the fire just as well as He could make others to live out of it. I have no doubt that, if there are inhabitants there, they enjoy the heat.

In a spiritual sense, at any rate, we know that men
who live near to Jesus dwell in the divine flame of
love.

Here is Spurgeon, then, who would not be shaken in
the discovery of life forms outside earth. It would be no
'death blow' to him if even on nearby Mercury life was
found. He would only find it interesting and no doubt
discover in it an illustration of the truth of the gospel.

A final point

My concern in this chapter is that people in the scientific community and those who are influenced by it
would not dismiss or reject Jesus based on a faulty notion like the one expressed by Mark Lupisella.

Whatever may or may not be 'out there' cannot
damage or compromise the gospel of our Lord Jesus
Christ. To think so is error, and error of the most dangerous kind.

Jesus himself must be studied, the probes must be
sent out to investigate him, the telescopes must be aimed
in his direction. Then he will be found because the promise is that if we seek him we will find him.

Notes
1. Michael McCabe's article 'Idea of Alien Life Gaining Credibility' in the San Francisco Chronicle, 2 December 1999, p. A3.
2. Zondervan Publishing House, p. 425.

3.
The big gamble

3.
The big gamble

Most mornings I have to wait in line at the 7-11 store to buy my newspaper while people place their bets with the California lottery. A woman, anticipating my impatience as she took an inordinate amount of time making her choice, turned to me and defended her purchase of twenty lottery tickets. 'I have to have something to look forward to.'

I knew what she meant. All day long she could daydream about the millions she might win and the very notion of it would carry her through the day.

The woman at the store was not putting all of her money on the proverbial 'line', but many are putting far more than money on the line.

The big gamble

There is indeed an even bigger gamble than the lottery — many are gambling that the grave is the end, the absolute end of life. My guess is that this is the most used, albeit unnamed, gamble of them all. The cessation of all life at the termination of the biological functions of the organism — this is the great hope of the godless. Nearly everyone who is committed to atheistic evolutionary schemes is hoping for this. These people reject any form of reincarnation taught by Hinduism or Buddhism as well. (I have observed, however, that they do not oppose eastern religious ideas with as much energy as they do traditional Christian doctrines about the after-life.)

The 'life ends at death' theory is powerful because of the abundance of evidence that seems to support it. And I admit there is plenty of information about the theory of random occurrences flowing from the physical sciences that seem to negate the necessity of a creator God. Evolutionary theories and hypotheses are being confirmed, apparently, regularly. These new discoveries seem to promise that any objections to evolutionary theories will be met at some point or another. There is no question but that the doctrine of life as a random event that ends at death is attractive and powerful.

Where is the proof?

No one committed to a 'life ends at death' doctrine can be absolutely sure of the truth of it. It is an article of faith and nothing more. It is a gamble and the stakes, of course, are monstrously high — nothing less than eternity.

Suppose the theories that account for life postulated by agnostics and atheists are absolutely correct. Who is to say there is not a God who started it all? Even if the universe and the earth are as old as the theories suggest, does this do away with God? Certainly not! And again, if creatures resembling modern humans date back a million years, does this mean God did not specially create Adam and Eve? Certainly not! Science, many contend, can only discover the handiwork of God. Science is not intended to be a means of judging whether or not there is a God. Besides, experience teaches that scientific 'truth' has a habit of changing. God, on the other hand, does not change. It is unwise to wager eternal life on presumptions founded on scientific theories.

Would a miracle do?

Jesus told the story of a rich man who died and went to hell. Lazarus, a beggar who had lain at the rich man's door, also died but he went to heaven. The rich man wanted God (Abraham in the story) to send Lazarus to his family to warn them about the terrible place of punishment and anguish. But Lazarus was not allowed to warn the rich man's family. God reminded him that they had the Scriptures and that even if someone returned from the dead they would not believe (Luke 16:19-31).

It is easy to sympathize with the rich man — he thought a miracle would be persuasive. And it might also seem like it would be for the 'life ends at death' devotee. How many people have sworn: 'If I could just have a sign, if I could just know for sure, then I would believe.'

If God would only grant miracles it would make it easier for all people to believe — or so it seems. But God's way is faith that is placed in Jesus of Nazareth, who died in our place on the cross and then rose from the dead. Trust, surrender, love — this is how it works. If God were to reveal himself through miracles all the time (sometimes he does perform miracles but usually only to those who already believe) then he would be just another fact. We do not have a personal relationship with facts.

The end of the story

The woman at the store buying the lottery tickets was not making an all-or-nothing bet, but so many are wagering eternity that the grave will be their end. Like the rich man, they will be shocked to find they lost their bet. But it will be discovered only after the debt has been collected. Hell is a truth learned too late.

4.
Bill's pain

4.
Bill's pain

The last week of October 1999 I drove to Yuba City, California, USA, to be with some former high school friends for two days of 'catching up'. On the morning of the second day, Bill said he did not feel well. We thought it might be indigestion since we had eaten hot peppers at a Mexican restaurant the night before. Nearly two hours passed and his pain grew steadily worse.

Bill has periodic bouts with skin cancer and has had surgery to control sleep apnoea, so he handles pain well — but this pain was making him very uncomfortable. The decision was taken to go to the emergency department at Rideout Memorial Hospital in Yuba City.

We arrived at the hospital about 10.30am, by which time Bill's pain had him pleading for relief; but none was provided... Nurses and a doctor prodded and poked Bill, hoping to determine the cause of the pain. After three hours a nurse finally showed up with a hypodermic needle and gave Bill a light dose of a pain-killing drug. It barely touched the pain.

I watched my friend in agony for two more hours. He pleaded for another shot. The doctor and the nurses seemed indifferent, going about their business, as the emergency department was quite busy. At one point I confronted the head nurse and pleaded for Bill myself. I did not prevail; Bill continued to writhe in pain.

After a number of tests were run, a surgeon came into the room and told Bill he would have to have his appendix removed. He leaned over the bed and said, 'Sorry about the pain, but if there is no pain we would be hard put to find the cause. Painkillers hide disease.'

Bill came through the operation fine and is back at work, although somewhat later than first projected because the appendix was gangrenous. Much more delay might have cost Bill his life. But I learned something about pain and gospel preaching.

When unconverted people hear the gospel they will sometimes feel rather uncomfortable. The Holy Spirit's convicting of sin can be most unpleasant. Hearing that repentance to God and faith in the Lord Jesus Christ is required may be quite shocking to the system. Pain! — a deep, existential, soulful, pain may be the result. I have often seen this and too often I have sought to bring comfort to the anguished sinner. I offered counselling, suggested therapy, made affirming and supporting declarations. I supplied a painkiller not fully realizing that sin was causing the pain and that radical, spiritual, surgery was needed to cut out the deadly disease.

A woman who had been attending my church in Miller Avenue for two or more years made an appointment to see me. She had realized she was not a Christian and was greatly disturbed about it. As she sat in my office, she cried, describing the stress she was under and saying she was at her wit's end. My response was to comfort her. I opened my Bible to Romans 10:9-10 and read to her about confessing Jesus as Lord. I asked her if she wanted to confess Jesus and she said she did. I asked, 'Do you believe God raised him from the dead?' She said, 'Yes.' 'Okay then, confess that Jesus is your Lord.' She did.

That was five years ago. Within one month of that meeting she left the church never to return. I have maintained contact with her, sending sermon tapes and newsletters through the post. She was never converted. I gave her false and dangerous comfort. I did not see it at the time; I thought I was helping.

The process of conversion to Jesus may be difficult. Certainly we know that human childbirth is painful to the mother and the baby usually comes out crying. Would we expect anything less in new birth? Sometimes people enter the kingdom of God violently. They struggle with coming to the light that exposes their sin, then they are confronted with letting go of sin that may have been in place for decades, and then finally to see their need to trust in Jesus for salvation.

As I preach the riches of God's grace and mercy in Christ, I have to allow the Holy Spirit to operate; and some conditions are worse than others. In any case, I must not be too quick to comfort, as I do not want to mask the pain that is an indication of the disease. Physical pain will return when the affects of the drug wear off, but the falsely comforted sinner may never again feel the pain. Then the condition is worse than before.

5.
Is sin a disease?

5.
Is sin a disease?

Sin is different from physical or emotional disease. The concept of sin implies personal responsibility for one's actions. Sin has to do with right and wrong. Sin presumes a holy God who, as Creator, has the authority to establish his law and punish lawbreakers. In the Bible, this holy God has revealed both what sin is and the fact that it must be atoned for and forgiven. Sin is not a disease that can be treated by medical science. Medication and therapy will not 'cure' sin. Therefore, redefining sin as a disease is a great mistake.

The issue

Increasingly however, medical and psychiatric professionals, social engineers, representatives of the pharmaceutical industry, and politicians are convinced that one type of disease or another is at the root of many, if not most, of our personal and social problems. Even Alcoholic's Anonymous, an organization I greatly respect, considers alcoholism a disease.

Diseases can be medically treated. Usually there are signs and symptoms, then a diagnosis is made, and finally treatment is offered. Treatment by medication is becoming so ubiquitous that we are in danger of becoming like the society depicted by George Orwell in *1984* where everyone was required to swallow his daily dose of soma.

We are becoming too comfortable with the notion that people with problems are diseased, and correspondingly then we are amenable to the use of mind-altering drug therapies (often accompanied with psychotherapy).

At the same time, many recoil at the 'accusation' that they are sinners. This was definitely true of me; and, as a long-time preacher of the gospel, I can say without hesitation that it is true of many people who consider themselves Christians.

A personal story

My brother Gary was an army combat engineer in Vietnam in 1966-67. Prior to the end of his tour there he encountered some serious trouble and was sent to a hospital in Japan diagnosed with a psychiatric illness. After his return home, he regularly took medication and visited a Veterans Administration psychologist. His medication consisted of inter-muscular injections of some type of drug. My brother eventually resisted the medication because he was unable to function at the part-time plumbing job he had found. Fearing he would be fired, he stopped taking the injections. Within several weeks, however, in extreme desperation, he killed himself.

I value the scientific advances made in the medical field and in no way disparage modern medicine and psychiatry. I also concede that there are instances where drug therapy must be applied. Many people are greatly helped at some point in their lives through the use of therapy and drugs, either singlely or in combination. But, to attempt to turn sin into disease is an error, a most dangerous error indeed.

Sin: an abusive term?

To many non-Christians, sin is a discomforting, even irritating word, and I imagine most people would prefer it to disappear from common usage. Is it possible that the use of the word in public may one day be considered abusive? My experience demonstrates that this might be the case. Of course, there are those people, like some of the more extrovert television evangelists, who will use the word in a strident, unloving manner. But however it is used, in whatever context, hackles rise at its mere mention. It is a stretch of the imagination at this point in history to predict that a lawsuit might result from the use of the word, but it may well come to that if current trends continue.

The 'S' word

At the same time that some people are growing resistant to the 'S' word, they are becoming comfortable with a disease paradigm. There is no shame or guilt in admitting: 'I have a disease that makes me act this way, I need treatment, I need help.' And this may be an accurate evaluation. But if a problem is actually moral in nature, to make a misdiagnosis is dangerous. To face up to guilt and shame may actually be the healthiest course to take. But avoiding personal, moral responsibility often feels like the path of least resistance and therefore is an attractive coping mechanism. It even comes close to the old excuse: 'The devil made me do it.'

Sin — a spiritual disease?

Sin is a spiritual disease. It is like a cancer that works, usually unseen, inside a person. The symptoms of the sinful condition are the breaking of the laws of God, a rebellion against God and his Word, the Bible. Sin, when it has wreaked its havoc, yields death; and not merely physical death. Sin separates a person from God and heaven for ever and must result in the unforgiven person being placed into hell. Obviously sin is worse than any type of disease. For example, even if a Christian dies of a physical disease he will still spend eternity with his Lord in heaven. On the other hand, a person who is healthy in every way and yet rejects Jesus and his gospel will die and be excluded from God's presence.

Do dysfunctional people commit more sin than 'normal' people? I don't believe so, except to state that dysfunctional people's problems may be more apparent and may get them into more trouble with society. The Bible does not teach that only 'troubled' people are sinners and fall short of the glory of God. No, we are all under the power and penalty of sin, whether we are mentally healthy or not.

Alienation from God yields a life of meaninglessness, loneliness and despair. A person in rebellion against God will often experience depression, anxiety and other mental/emotional symptoms as well as psychogenic physical illnesses. Although those symptoms may appear to be amenable to medical and psychiatric therapies, they are not.

Recall the medical model of disease-therapy: examination of signs and symptoms; diagnosis; and treatment. A person suffering from alienation from God may present various signs and symptoms of mental and psychogenic problems. But if the true, underlying cause of those symptoms is not recognized, then the diagnosis will be wrong and no type of medical or psychiatric treatment will prove effective.

A terrible misdiagnosis

If we are fooled into thinking our problems, personal and social, can be exclusively treated by medical and psychiatric professionals, then we will be guilty of an awful misdiagnosis and the real disease will continue undetected. Certainly disease is a major human problem and people are helped through the prescription of drugs and use of therapy. And yes, we are fortunate to have these tools available. But it is as the old proverb says, 'We cannot see the forest for the trees.' The forest is sin and even a good psychiatrist and prozac, the very best medicine has to offer, will not bring a cure for the disease of sin.

The accurate diagnosis and remedy

Disease, despite its awful role in human history, is neither the fundamental nor ultimate problem. Sin is. And God himself has a remedy for sin. The Bible teaches that God the Father has sent his Son Jesus to be the means for the forgiveness of sins. On the cross, Jesus took the full punishment for the believer's sin upon himself. Jesus' suffering, death and resurrection is the only remedy provided by God for sin and its consequences. Jesus himself then is the only 'treatment' for spiritual disease and alienation. The Christian solution for sin is both humble and elegant: a simple trusting in Jesus for forgiveness.

Sin must be acknowledged; this is the first step towards spiritual health. The first spiritual truth I learned was that I had sinned against God and stood guilty before him. Yes, admitting my sin was not pleasant and I resisted doing so for some considerable period of time. At the same time, I had a growing understanding that Jesus had died for my sin. The darkness of the reality of my sin was being countered by the light of God's grace and mercy. The sharp sense of my sin was the pain that led me to the healing of Jesus' atoning work on the cross.

Our God, the Great Physician, delights in forgiveness of sin and takes no pleasure in punishing the sinner. When we experience that forgiveness we know God for the loving and good God he is. Sin, even the word itself, loses its power over us because we know its terrible scourge has been removed for ever.

6.
Lyman Beecher: How he died

6.

Lyman Beecher: How he died

In *Preaching and Preachers* Dr David Martyn Lloyd-Jones referred to Lyman Beecher's (1775-1863) correspondence with and about Asahel Nettleton, the great preacher of the first half of the second Great Awakening in America. Beecher himself was greatly used of God in the early part of that awakening in his local church, and, throughout his long ministry, stood firmly for a Reformed faith over many controversies and trials. Lloyd-Jones recommended Beecher's biography for an understanding of the controversy between Nettleton and C. G. Finney over the 'new measures' employed by Finney. The book was published by Harper & Brothers Publishers in 1865 and the two volumes and more than 1000 pages reveals much about the life and ministry of Lyman Beecher. In reading it I found much more than I was looking for, particularly in the period before Beecher died. Four incidents especially stand out.

Firstly, in retirement he attended Plymouth Church of Boston, USA, and during one of the last times he ever spoke to a group, he 'said feebly, "If God should tell me that I might choose" (and then hesitating, as if it might seem like unsubmissiveness to the divine will) — "that is, if God said that it was his will that I should choose whether to die and go to heaven, or to begin my life over again and work once more" (straightening himself up, and his eye kindling, with his finger lifted up), "I would enlist again in a minute!"' (vol. 2, p. 552).

As a preacher of the gospel I thrilled to read those words. Beecher, aware of his diminished capacity, longed to depart and be with his Lord. Yet his love for his God-commissioned work was such that he would gladly do it all again. The great preacher, neither cynical nor discouraged by the unfaithfulness and error around him, would come into the pulpit and plead with sinners. Though a warrior, often wounded, he was ready to take the field anew. Beecher's 'feeble' words will long stay with me.

Secondly, a friend, hoping to rouse Beecher out of a long period of 'vacancy', asked him: 'Dr Beecher, tell us what is the greatest of all things.' The answer, I quickly admit, I have memorized since I know I will repeat it often: 'It is not theology, it is not controversy, but it is to save souls.' Not that theology was unimportant; in fact, Beecher was a staunch defender of the faith once delivered to the saints. Furthermore, Beecher did not shy away from the controversies of his day. But the one great thing, which thrills me also, is to preach the gospel that sinners might be converted. This saying, too, I will not soon forget (p. 555).

Thirdly, Beecher wanted to be buried next to his dear friend and long-time pastoral colleague, a Dr Taylor of Connecticut. The biography is replete with references to Taylor, and contains dozens of their letters to each other. Though Dr Beecher's memory was nearly gone, he would remember his old friend and one day declared that he wanted to be buried next to him. He reasoned,

'The young men [the students] will come and see where Brother Taylor and I are buried, and it will do them good' (p. 555).

Beecher's burying place would be, he supposed, a last sermon of inspiration and encouragement to his students, probably referring to the students of Lane Seminary, into which Beecher had poured so much of his life and ministry. Even in that last detail, a resting-place, Beecher had his eye on the glory of God. Could I be so concerned for the kingdom of God?

Fourthly, knowing his earthly life was quickly coming to a close, he examined his own heart to see whether he was truly converted or not. His son and chief biographer, Charles Beecher, writes, 'Such was his sense of his imperfectness before the divine law, and such his profound humility before God, and such his sense of the solemnity of that great change that settles all for ever, that he seldom or never spoke of his own condition with assurance, but only of prevailing hope on the whole' (p. 557).

Twice, however, at the very end, his daughter Harriet Beecher Stowe reported that he quoted these words of Paul: 'I have fought a good fight, I have finished my course, I have kept the faith; henceforth there is laid up for me a crown, which God, the righteous Judge, will give me in that day'; and added, 'that is my testimony; write it down; that is my testimony' (p. 557).

The examination completed, Lyman Beecher found his hope to be sure. I likewise hope, if possible, to make a similar examination now and then. For I, like Dr Beecher, know that there is one great and important thing and that is to know the Saviour who is the resurrection and the life.

7.
Taking away hope

7.
Taking away hope

The pro-gay position among some segments of the Christian community effectively deprives the homosexual of hope. These persons may be thinking they are reaching out in love to the gay community, but to theorize that a gay person is born that way and therefore cannot help being homosexual takes away hope. What may pass for a tolerant and accepting attitude among certain people in fact condemns a person to what many gay people will admit is an unhappy, even desperate, life. And it also abandons people committed to homosexual behaviour to a dreadful eternity as well.

A frightening passage

The passage I am about to quote is one that is feared, even hated, by pro-gay 'Christians'. It is a passage that has been vigorously attacked by pro-gay Bible commentators because of its powerful message. But it is a passage that is simple and clear in its meaning, and yet, in my view, holds out a great deal of hope for the homosexual. The first part of the passage states:

Do you not know that the wicked will not inherit the kingdom of God? Do not be deceived: Neither the sexually immoral nor idolaters nor adulterers nor male prostitutes nor homosexual offenders nor thieves nor the greedy nor drunkards nor slanderers nor swindlers will inherit the kingdom of God

(1 Corinthians 6:9-10).

I do not intend to browbeat anyone with the Bible. And I do not want to scare anyone either — I want to present the hope that all sinners have in Christ.

An examination of the passage

'Homosexual offenders' is a translation of the Greek word *arsenokoite*, a word that Paul made up (Paul made up or coined about 170 words that we find in his New Testament letters). The word he used is a combination of *arsenos* meaning 'male', and *koite* meaning 'bed' or 'couch'. Paul found these words in Leviticus 18:22 and Leviticus 20:13, in the Greek translation of the Old Testament called the Septuagint. The Levitical verses forbid and condemn homosexuality. Paul put the two words together because he wanted to describe men who had sex together. It is not homosexual prostitution or violent homosexual rape that the Law of Moses is concerned with as is so often presented by pro-gay writers. No, the language is clear and straightforward — homosexual offenders, or those who practise homosexuality, will not inherit the kingdom of God.

Homosexual behaviour is not the only sinful behaviour mentioned in the Corinthian passage. There is quite a long list and I find some of my own sins there, too. There are the heterosexuals who are immoral and adulterers who have sex outside of marriage with someone other than their spouse. There are those who worship gods who are no gods at all. There are thieves, greedy people, drunkards, slanderers, and swindlers listed — I find myself here. I have broken God's holy ordinance and therefore, barring a miracle, I will not inherit the kingdom of God. If God's Word is true, I am in desperate trouble.

Am I without hope?

Since I find my sin(s) plainly listed in the passage, am I then without hope? In one sense I have no hope for I cannot do anything about changing what has already happened, and, to make matters worse, I cannot be assured that I will not sin again sometime in the future. Though I do not want to sin and dishonour my Lord, it is more than likely that I will, because sin dwells within me (see 1 John 1:8 - 2:1-2). Yet I am not without hope; in fact, I am most hopeful. I know for a fact that Jesus has died in my place on the cross; I know he has taken all my sin upon himself, and that I can be forgiven, trusting in him as the Holy Spirit enables me. Certainly I can do nothing, but this Jesus, risen from the dead, has already done what I cannot do. Indeed, he gives me his righteousness, even though I do not deserve it at all. This is the good news, the gospel.

The proof of hope

Earlier I quoted 1 Corinthians 6:9-10. But I stopped short of the real point Paul was making to the believers in Corinth. We need now to look at verse 11 for it contains proof of our hope.

> And that is what some of you were. But you were washed, you were sanctified, you were justified in the name of the Lord Jesus Christ and by the Spirit of our God.

In that Corinthian church were people like me — guilty of many sins, addicted to some, helplessly in the control of others. Yet, something happened to them and Paul used three words to describe it — *washed, sanctified,* and *justified.*

Washed means being granted forgiveness. This involves a work of the Holy Spirit in applying the blood Jesus shed on the cross to the sinner. With the shedding of blood there is the forgiveness of sin, even sin like my own, sin like homosexual behaviour, too. I cannot forgive my own sin neither can a church nor a priest nor a minister nor anyone nor anything else forgive sin; no, only Jesus' blood can wash away sin. Did Jesus die on the cross and shed his blood to then withhold it from those who seek him? Not at all; remember that Jesus is the one who came to call, not the righteous, but sinners to repentance. And the washing, the cleansing, of the blood of Jesus actually brings us to a place of repentance. Washed, clean, forgiven, this is more wonderful than anything can ever be.

Sanctified, then, means to be set aside as belonging to Jesus himself. It is the result of the washing — forgiven and cleansed of sin we are indwelt by the Holy Spirit. The sanctified are embraced by the Father and adopted into his own family. God's Holy Spirit actually lives within us because that which prevented his doing so was overcome when our sins were forgiven. It is completely the work of God. He sets us aside, makes us holy, and begins to work within us both to will and to work for his good pleasure — which takes a whole lifetime.

Justified might well have been mentioned first, or second, because it is the experience of conversion or the new birth. It happens as we are washed and sanctified. Where one begins and the other ends we do not know. There is a mystery to it all, though it is very real at the same time. 'Justified' might be defined as the sinner being restored to a condition of purity, as though no sin had ever been committed. It is by faith, it is grace. It is all a gift. Faith is a gift, we really have none of it in ourselves, rather, it is given to us. This is what we mean by grace — forgiveness and eternal life freely given despite the fact that we are unworthy. This is illustrated for us in the words 'new birth'. We did not effect our own physical birth and so we cannot effect our spiritual birth. It is all a gift of God, not based on any kind or manner of work.

Giving back hope

Those who accept the notion that they were born homosexual and that it is in their very nature to be homosexual may find hope in the words of Paul and in the experience of some of the Christians in the church at Corinth. There were homosexuals there, and they had turned away from homosexual behaviour, though they might not have become heterosexuals (some today at any rate experience a change in their sexual orientation but others do not, so it is not unreasonable to state that such might have been the case in Corinth).

A special appeal

To those who have loved ones who are gay, perhaps a son or daughter, I appeal to you that you do not take away their hope by agreeing that they cannot help but engage in homosexual activity.

There is a powerful tendency to overlook what the Scriptures teach and adopt a pro-gay stance thinking we are standing with and supporting our gay loved ones. Many do this. It is, in the long run, better to love the person, be supportive in whatever means possible, all the while refusing to validate the sinful behaviour. This 'tough love' may well prove to be both hopeful and redemptive.

Words of hope

The pro-gay movement unwittingly takes away hope but the promise of the Scriptures gives it back. The following grand words of Paul provide for us a most fitting close to this chapter:

May the God of hope fill you with all joy and peace
as you trust in him, so that you may overflow with
hope by the power of the Holy Spirit

(Romans 15:13).

8.
What is happening to hell?

8.
What is happening to hell?

I enjoy preaching on heaven; I dislike preaching on hell. Over the last fourteen years I have preached on hell once. Of course, I mention the doctrine every so often, but always in passing. This, I am convinced, is an error on my part, especially since the doctrine is rapidly falling into disrepute among those who once embraced it.

The doctrine

As a doctrine, hell is solidly biblical. Certainly Jesus is abundantly clear on the reality of hell. In Matthew 25:41, Jesus states: 'Then he will say to those on his left, "Depart from me, you who are cursed, into the eternal fire prepared for the devil and his angels."' Jesus concluded his remarks on the 'sheep and goats judgement' by saying, 'Then they will go away to eternal punishment, but the righteous to eternal life' (Matthew 25:46). Note that both heaven and hell are eternal. Those who believe in annihilation cannot have it both ways; if heaven is eternal, hell must be as well. (For further research on the subject see Matthew 5:29; 8:11-12; Mark 9:43; Luke

16:19-31; 2 Thessalonians 1:9; Jude 6; Revelation 14:10-11; 20:10; 21:8.)

The biblical doctrine on hell has long been standard in mainstream Christianity. In his sermon 'The Great Assize' John Wesley said, 'It follows, that either the punishment lasts for ever, or the reward too will come to an end; no, never, unless God could come to an end, or His mercy and truth could fail.' John Calvin wrote: 'But the whole Scripture proclaims that there will be no end of the happiness of the elect, or the punishment of the reprobate.'[1]

Cults and sects

The Christian-based cults, the Jehovah's Witnesses, Mormons, Christian Scientists, and so on, deny the existence of an eternal hell and substitute some other circumstance that awaits the 'non-believer'. This seeming 'reasonable and charitable' approach is one reason for the appeal of these cults. 'Ah, the hated, unfair, and unreasonable doctrine of the professors of Christendom is shown to be false,' the cults' ministers boast to the prospect.

The Adventists, a sect of Christianity (not now so doctrinally aberrant to earn the designation 'cult'), have long stressed the theory of annihilation. Their view is that life for the unconverted ends for ever. (The Jehovah's Witnesses were influenced by this Adventist idea and changed it only slightly — Jehovah God slays all non-Witnesses and unfaithful Witnesses.) In any case, both the cults and certain so-called Christian sects like the Adventists deny the biblical teaching of an eternal punishment in hell.

The church growth movement

Hell is not faring well with those committed to the church growth movement either. The doctrine simply will not help get people into the pews. Whether the ministers within the movement believe it or not is unknown, and irrelevant. The determinant is that embarrassing doctrines must be hidden from view, as they do not serve the greater purpose — getting people in the door and seated in the pew. The result, though, is a slighting if not a downright rejection of the truth. And this will ultimately serve neither the seeker nor the unchurched because they will not realize their desperate need to come to Christ.

Summary

How the cults operate and the contemporary efforts to attract the unchurched we already know about. However, there is something else afoot that is even more dangerous.

Leave it to ignorance

Philip Yancey, noted and respected among American evangelical Christians, admits in an article titled 'The Encyclopedia of Theological Ignorance'[2] that doctrines like an eternal hell bother him. He asks: 'Will hell really involve an eternity of torment?' Essentially he says that hell is a marginal doctrine, obscure, and not plain. He wonders why the Bible does not give clear answers to the marginal doctrines.

Yancey differentiates between doctrines that are clear and those that are not. He appears theologically orthodox in general, but indicates that what the Bible says about hell is unclear. He would include the doctrine of hell in his 'Encyclopedia of Theological Ignorance' as he would the subject of infant salvation. Yancey says that the issue of infant salvation is unclear in the Bible (and maybe it is), therefore we should trust a loving and merciful God to do what is right and not attempt to clear up this marginal doctrine.

Hell is to be taken in the same way. The Bible is then, according to Yancey, unclear on the subject. This is amply demonstrated in the conclusion of his article.

> I must insist that the most important questions about heaven and hell — who goes where, whether there are second chances, what form the judgements and rewards take, intermediate states after death — are opaque at best. Increasingly, I am grateful for that ignorance and grateful that the God who revealed himself in Jesus is the one who knows the answers.

Opaque?

By 'opaque' Yancey means unclear, and he means the same when referring to the doctrine of hell. Yancey believes in heaven and hell, but in a way that negates or blunts their reality. A person persuaded by Yancey might well reason: 'Hmmm, the doctrine of hell, I don't have to take it seriously, I don't have to believe in it, I don't have to teach or preach it, I don't have to warn anyone of the danger of going there, I don't have to fear it myself — because it is not a clear Bible doctrine. Yes, I will leave it all up to God and, after all, he is merciful and loving.'

What has Yancey done? He has muddled an important doctrine. He has told the watchman to come down from the tower because there is no enemy. It is as if to say: 'Why all this scary talk about judgement and hell? It is not clear, and of course, whatever is not clear we should disregard and assign to "The Encyclopedia of Theological Ignorance".'

Accountability

Can we accept what Yancey advocates?

Personally, I cannot; but on one hand it would be nice if I could. If I could relax about the doctrine of hell, if I could convince myself that is a marginal doctrine, I would not need to warn and plead with the unconverted. I would reduce the risk of scaring them away. My reputation among the unconverted and especially the christianized might improve, but I cannot do it. I do not like the idea of hell any more than any other Christian. But the Scriptures teach it; the doctrine is beyond question. To say that the doctrine of hell is opaque is to both impugn the integrity of Jesus and deny the authority of Scripture. Worst of all, it gives the unconverted false hope and comfort. How very dangerous; how very awful.

Emotional and personal reasons to reject the doctrine of hell

Hell is a doctrine that Christians find difficult, not for theological reasons often, nor biblical reasons, but for emotional and personal reasons. I understand this.

My mother, who gave me life and loved me unconditionally, died not trusting in Jesus. As best I could I shared the gospel with her but she steadfastly rejected it. Moreover my wife's family, siblings, parents and grandparents are strangers to the promise of eternal life in Christ. So, I have many reasons why I might want to obscure the doctrine of hell. How comforting it might seem to downplay hell, perhaps develop a theology of second chances, accept the notion that beloved family members could yet find safety and salvation in heaven apart from grace, or even suggest some sort of universalism. While one of these might ease some pain and anxiety, it would do no one any good.

A dear friend recently confessed to me that he was terribly upset that his father might die in his sins and be condemned to hell. I was tempted to comfort him by minimizing the reality of hell. Would it have helped? Would it have been the honest thing to do? As Christians we must face these hard truths. We did not make them up and whether we believe them or not does not, cannot, alter the truth.

A clear and present duty

Preachers (and we are all preachers) of the whole coun-
sel of God and the fulness of the gospel have to warn of
hell. However unpleasant it is, however many people
designate us hopeless literalists, the truth must be made
clear. Ours is a higher duty than to falsely comfort the
unconverted as Philip Yancey has done.

Preachers of the gospel have been made watchmen
who will give account of their ministry.

> When I say to the wicked, 'O wicked man, you
> will surely die,' and you do not speak out to dis-
> suade him from his ways, that wicked man will
> die for his sin, and I will hold you accountable for
> his blood. But if you do warn the wicked man to
> turn from his ways and he does not do so, he will
> die for his sin, but you will be saved yourself
> (Ezekiel 33:8-9).

To and from

If I did not believe that the unconverted would end up
in hell I doubt I would preach much of a gospel. What
would be the point? If there is nothing to be saved *from*
why preach a gospel of salvation? Someone might counter, 'Well it is still better to have faith and be positive
even if it is for this life only.' How can I, however, follow the example of Jesus and do anything he com-
manded me in this life if he has lied to me about heaven
and hell? No, we are saved *to* and *from* something. We

are saved *to* be in Christ now and enjoy the abundant life he gives us, and then finally *to* be with him in heaven. And we are saved *from* being separated *from* him for ever in hell. This is an essential part of the gospel.

What happens to hell is not marginal

What will the minister preach who does not believe in hell? There will be sermons about justice, self-improvement, the poor and disadvantaged, and more — all important subjects. But since there is a judgement that follows the resurrection of the just and the unjust, it will be an incomplete ministry. As Jesus said, 'What good will it be for a man if he gains the whole world, yet forfeits his soul?' (Matthew 16:26).

I am not suddenly going to become a 'hell-fire and brimstone' preacher. But I will preach on it, I will warn of a terrible judgement upon all those outside of Christ that will surely result in an eternal hell. I will so preach because it is the truth, and people need to know the truth so that they would seek him out and be found by him.

Notes
1. *The Institutes*, Book III, chapter 25, section 5.
2. *Christianity Today*, 6 September 1999, Vol. 43, No. 10, p. 120.

9.
It amazes me

9.
It amazes me

It amazes me that anyone around here comes to Christ at all. And it is no surprise that less than 3% of my fellow citizens of Marin County, California, USA, attend church services on Easter Sunday.

From the newspaper

Here are thumbnail sketches of items I read in the *San Francisco Chronicle* recently. Two teenage brothers in Redding, California, shot two homosexuals to death because it was their 'Christian' duty to do so. An ex-Protestant minister was in town to promote his new book on Tibetan Buddhism. A Catholic priest in Santa Rosa, arrested for molesting altar boys over the course of fifteen years, made a plea bargain with the district attorney's office. A Baptist pastor in the South Bay, convicted of embezzling church funds, was sent to state prison. The daughter of a Protestant minister, after recovering lost childhood memories, sued her now retired father for sexual abuse. A professional football player active in Christian ministry received three years probation for drug use and sales. An archaeologist made fun of the Bible's account of Noah's Ark in a lecture at a local college. A school board in a southern state passed a resolution prohibiting fundamentalists from displaying the Ten Commandments in schoolrooms. An Alabama judge's decision that evolution cannot be taught in the schools was overturned. The pastor of a Pentecostal church in Oakland disappeared with the money raised to get the congregation ready for Y2K. A local radio preacher announced that Jesus would not return on 1 January 2000 but on 1 January 2001. You don't want to hear about the previous week.

It amazes me that anyone is ever converted around here. But, once in a while, someone is. I know this is California, but what is reported in the *Chronicle* makes newspapers across the country. And what I reported about the newspaper items is nothing compared with the crazy things shown on 'Christian' television and radio (I won't discourage you by describing them). Then there are the surrounding churches themselves. When I talk about it to others in different parts of the country they think I am making it up or am at least exaggerating. Well, believe me or not, here is some of it.

Local churches

First, let me tell you how I know. Some people around here, although very few, are church shoppers, that is, they shop around for a church to belong to. Or, they attend churches for short periods due to some special lecture series or concert that is given. Or, a disgruntled former member returns with tales to tell. The combination of these gives me a good idea of what is happening. But more pertinent, I know most of the ministers around here and occasionally meet with them.

Several pastors of local churches do not consider themselves Christians and say so from the pulpit. One is a Hindu, another is a self-described agnostic, and a third is a 'post-modern' seeker after truth wherever it might be found. I am not telling tales here, nor am I passing on negative information. These pastors are proud of their spiritual attainments. Their churches are the largest and wealthiest in southern Marin County.

The homeless

Then there are the homeless. One wears a red hooded sweatshirt so that he will always be covered in the blood of Jesus. I have seen him recently in front of the 7-11 store with the hood pulled closed across his face. Many local people know he does this to keep the demons out (he has made this clear himself and does so as a 'witness'). He imagines that he is a glamour expert and frequently approaches women with tips on how to make themselves look beautiful for Jesus.

Another is continually running for various local political offices and on the ballot paper he lists his occupation as 'minister'. On one television interview, panel discussion, or debate after another he makes a mockery of Christianity and the Bible with his strange and deranged comments. He is widely known for carrying around a huge copy of a Bible that was printed in the early 1500s.

I am not proud of this in a peculiar way, I am not trying to raise money to combat the evil around me, and I do not consider myself to be a better minister than any other. It is simply that given it all I am amazed that anyone is ever converted.

Blind and bound

Another reason why I am amazed anyone ever trusts in Jesus is that Satan has blinded the eyes (the mind) of the unconverted, as described by Paul in 2 Corinthians 4:4. Satan, the god of this age, blinds in ways we do not understand. Jesus said Satan uses pretended signs and wonders in order to deceive (Matthew 24:24).

Our sin also keeps us from salvation. Because of this we hate the light of Jesus and will not come to him out of fear that our sins will be exposed (John 3:19-21). Paul says that sin produces spiritual death, so we cannot know anything of Jesus and his truth (Ephesians 2:1; 1 Corinthians 1:18; and 2:14).

It is amazing grace

It amazes me that anyone is ever converted. When I think of it too much I feel discouraged. And I do not see things getting any better (barring an awakening). But even without revivals and awakenings, some are being converted. I see it in my own church at Miller Avenue. In fact, God is constantly calling to himself those he has ordained to eternal life. I take great courage, hope and confidence from Acts 13:48, which states: 'all who were appointed for eternal life believed'. Though Paul's fellow Jews rejected the gospel, others, Gentiles in this case, did come to Jesus.

Jesus 'came to seek and to save what was lost' (Luke 19:10). He searches for us like the shepherd does for the lost sheep, the woman does for the lost coin, and when found receives us as the father does his lost son.

It is not my practice to wring my hands and lament the lack of success of the gospel. My task is to preach the gospel and know that God will save those whom he will. No one can come to Jesus unless he or she is drawn by the Father, but by the preaching of Jesus the Father does just that. 'Faith comes from hearing the message, and the message is heard through the word of Christ' (Romans 10:17).

What God did for me he will do for others. Despite my deadness, blindness, fear and error, he saved me. Yes, it amazes me!

10.
The real reason

10.

The real reason

For nearly thirty years I assumed a person could decide to become a Christian. However, it became clear that salvation was on the basis of grace through faith — gifts of God. This is evident from many passages of Scripture, such as Ephesians 2:8-9: 'For it is by grace you have been saved, through faith — and this not from yourselves, it is the gift of God — not by works, so that no one can boast.'

Faith and grace

I knew grace was a gift of God, but I had assumed faith rose out of the individual. I did not see that faith was a gift as well. But grace comes through faith and both are gifts. Faith cannot be a work or grace could not be grace. But this is more of a problem for many than I imagined! Why does the preaching of grace encounter so much hostility?

The real reason

The real reason is fear: fear that something so vital is beyond our control. Salvation, forgiveness, eternal life, the ultimate issues, all come through grace; they are given and cannot be acquired. So, then, what if God does not give them? What if God chooses to predestine to hell rather than heaven? It is a fearful prospect, or so it appears at first. But it is fear, perhaps demonically inspired fear, which is behind the hostility directed towards the good message of grace.

The fear of God

The Scriptures teach that the fear of God is the beginning of wisdom. The fear of God encouraged in the Bible is a respect, honour and reverence for almighty God. Fear of grace, though, is entirely different. This fear reasons: 'If I cannot choose God and he does not choose me, I am lost.' This is a great and terrible fear.

Good news!

It is good news that I cannot choose God. It is good news that God chooses me. Why? It is simply because I cannot believe. Not only am I dead in my trespasses and sins, but the best I can do as far as faith is concerned is to generate within myself some measure of positive thinking. Though positive thinking is often presented as the nature of faith, it is not at all. And I cannot do it in any case. I may be able to for a while, but I soon give way to doubt and pessimism. I cannot stay focused in my thinking. So then if my salvation depends on my ability to have this kind of faith, I am doomed and will be gripped with a powerful fear.

Love replaces fear

Love and fear are opposites. Remember the song: 'Jesus loves me, this I know, for the Bible tells me so.' Not only does God love me but he also does not wish me to perish but to come to him for forgiveness. He is actually seeking sinners; he is knocking on the door calling out our name. He has come to seek and save those who are lost. 'This is love: not that we loved God but that he loved us and sent his Son as an atoning sacrifice for our sins' (1 John 4:10); and 'But God demonstrates his own love for us in this: While we were still sinners, Christ died for us' (Romans 5:8). The truth is, then, that God's love overcomes our fear.

Come to Jesus

Here is both the heart of the matter and the reason for strong hope and confidence: 'All that the Father gives me will come to me, and whoever comes to me I will never drive away' (John 6:37). For that person who senses a fear of God and hostility towards grace welling up inside, this is not from God. Come to Jesus who is seeking you, loves you, and longs to be your Saviour.

11.
Soul confusion

11.
Soul confusion

On 16 March 1999 *Larry King Live*, an American television chat show, featured five panellists: Robert Thurman, professor of Buddhism Studies at Columbia University; Marianne Williamson, New Age author and spokesperson for the spiritistically channelled Course in Miracles; Rabbi David Aaron, expert on and proponent of Kabbalism, an occult/mystical/gnostic interpretation of Judaism; Deepak Chopra, charismatic spokesperson for a popular version of Hindu monistic thought; and Franklin Graham, head of Samaritans Purse, a Christian humanitarian organization, and son of Billy Graham, the renowned American evangelist.

What is the soul?

Though these five differed on many points, they seemed to be able to reach a consensus when it came to an understanding of 'soul'. In fact, Deepak Chopra voiced agreement with Graham's understanding of the soul. We have long heard Billy Graham say words like: 'You have a soul and it will go to heaven or hell when you die.'

According to this idea, the soul is a mysterious, spiritual and immortal part of the human being that leaves the cold, dead body at death. Those on Larry King's programme who believed in some form of reincarnation were able to agree together about the soul though, from their own traditions, they might have used other symbols to express the same thing.

Due to a revival of Greek philosophy in the fifth and sixth centuries A.D., Greek dualism infiltrated the Christian church mainly through the work of Thomas Aquinas and his *Summa Theologica*, which became the fountainhead of Catholic theology throughout the Dark Ages. Greek dualistic thought posits the theory that the mind, spirit and soul are good, even divine, while on the other hand, the body, flesh and matter are bad, the repository of evil. So it was the soul that mattered, the soul that needed saving; the body was simply a temporary prison for the soul.

Soul and self

Confusion concerning the nature of the soul has a powerful influence among the people of Mill Valley where I minister. Though the doctrine is not biblical, and is absent from the teaching of the early church, the idea that the soul is the focus of evangelistic efforts persists in many Christian traditions. Franklin Graham was concerned about the 'soul'. He should have been concerned about the whole person: body, mind, soul and spirit.

So many in my community believe in reincarnation that Graham's doctrine on the soul would not be troublesome for them. The soul? Well, they say, it needs purifying and experiences endless lifetimes anyway. These people do not like to think that they will be resurrected to stand before the judgement of God. 'My soul' is one thing; 'myself' is another.

Total resurrection

The biblical doctrine is one of bodily resurrection, not the floating away of an immortal soul. We are whole, integrated beings, though the Bible writers spoke variously of mind, heart, body, flesh, spirit and soul for the sake of emphasis. A person is all of these and more, a whole being responsible to God in the totality and indivisibility of his nature. What we are in total will be raised from the dead, either to eternal life or eternal death. We do not have immortality in and of ourselves. This truth is found in 1 Corinthians 15:53: 'For this corruptible must put on incorruption, and this mortal must put on immortality' (NKJV).

'Soul confusion' must be countered by the truth of the resurrection, even if it means parting from long-established ways of thinking and preaching. Let us not give the unconverted comfort by implying that they only have some ethereal 'soul' to be concerned about. They themselves may hear Jesus say, 'I never knew *you*. Away from me, you evildoers!' (Matthew 7:23).

12.
'You're a fundamentalist, aren't you?'

12.
'You're a fundamentalist, aren't you?'

I did not want to answer this question. No good would come of it anyway. Insults had been slung at me like a stone intended to wound. And this from a person who would not likely hurl a racial or ethnic epitaph at anyone.

People will accuse me of being a fundamentalist. I use the word 'accuse', which may not be a completely accurate description of the motive of every speaker, but it will sound like an accusation. Of course it is a label, a stereotype, that may reveal a deep-seated prejudice, even anger.

Few today know what the word means and most do not know the history of fundamentalism; it is simply a word used to diminish, demean and defame any Christian, whether he or she is a true fundamentalist or not, but who takes a stand for the Bible and Christ. Many Christians today would not appreciate the fundamentalist label being applied to them. The truth is, I do not like it myself.

Maybe I am one. If the original definition of fundamentalism is at issue, then indeed I am. At the beginning of the twentieth century, when anti-Christian liberalism was on the rise, some American conservative

Christians formulated the fundamentals of the faith in an attempt to counter the growing liberalism in the seminaries, denominational headquarters and churches. They declared a faith in the inspiration and authority of the Scriptures, and affirmed the deity, blood atonement, bodily resurrection and return of Jesus. There is nothing too controversial here, these are actually normal biblical views, that is, if one takes the Bible seriously at all. So why all the fuss about a 'fundamentalist'?

One problem was that the early fundamentalists began fighting among themselves as to who was the purest in doctrine and practice. It became quite vicious and the squabbles spilled over into the media. Then one group separated from another, followed by more splits, and the fabric of denominationalism was literally coming apart at the seams.

The liberal contingent of American Christianity even accused the fundamentalists of aiding and abetting the Axis powers during World War I because of the premillennial, dispensational end-times views. These views predicted a world getting worse and worse, and when this appeared to be happening, the fundamentalist scolded, 'See, I told you so.' It was certainly untrue that the fundamentalists supported America's enemies, but bad publicity has an impact regardless.

The famous 1925 Scopes Trial, otherwise known as the 'Monkey' trial, that pitted William Jennings Bryan, a Christian, against the renowned criminal lawyer, Clarence Darrow, was widely reported in the American press. The issue was whether evolution should be taught in the public schools. Bryan, an educated and gentlemanly defender of the Christian faith, and constantly defined as a fundamentalist, came off less than second best to Darrow, while fundamentalism and, indeed, all of Bible-believing Christianity, was made a laughing stock around the world. In fact, fundamentalists were often called Bryanites. Many Christians, I suspect, were scandalized by it all, and many more were turned from Christ altogether. This legacy continues into the modern age.

But there is still more. Some fundamentalist preachers, convinced they had the correct understanding of end-time prophecies, were sure that Mussolini (then later Hitler, and still later Stalin) was either the beast or the Antichrist of the Book of Revelation. After the process of history demonstrated the fallacy of such predictions, the fundamentalists lost a lot of credibility. Predictions are still being made, and fail, and continue to cause difficulties.

The fundamentalists developed social and political agendas as well. Soon, becoming a Christian also meant adopting a particular political affiliation or outlook — almost always of a conservative persuasion. Bible-believing Christians, it was thought, voted in a particular way. Fundamentalism took on science, too, hoping to counter the growing influence of evolution. This sometimes resulted in a pseudo-science, which was often laughable. Again, true Christians, according to hard-core fundamentalists, had to consider science to be an enemy to the faith.

Some fundamentalists thundered against things like hair and clothing styles, and various forms of popular entertainment; and, of course, they sharply rejected the use of alcohol and tobacco. Some historians blamed the fundamentalists as being responsible for the American Prohibition. Dancing was often singled out as being particularly evil, and the list goes on and on.

The fundamentalists were portrayed as 'meddling' with people's private lives and it did not go down well either in the media or over the back fence. 'Fundamentalist' came to be a word applied to people who were considered to be narrow, bigoted, backward, uneducated and boring.

Then there are the religious terrorists in more recent times: Hindus, Muslims, even Buddhists now, who are bombing people for some reason or another, and they are labelled either extremists, or more usually, fundamentalists. Every crazy cult, when they make the news, get the fundamentalist tag applied to them as well.

Does anyone want to be a fundamentalist? Most would say 'No!' And even the threat of being called a fundamentalist is enough to scare people away from churches, a desire to read the Bible, or entertain a spiritual thought that might be vaguely Christian in character. People will even be embarrassed to say anything that might connect them with things Christian and biblical, while at the same time, the same stigma is not attached to eastern, alternative and pagan religious practices and ideas. This is an unhappy, and unnecessary, state of affairs.

Since I am often asked if I am a fundamentalist, and since I have had to deal so often with the emotional stress of facing the fundamentalist branding in face to face confrontations, perhaps I could pass on some of my survival techniques.

The bottom line is: I don't much care what I am called personally. I would like to think my inner strength is well developed enough to take the name-calling. Jesus' strength is sufficient for me. He was accused of all sorts of things, so why should I think I would escape unthinking, unkind, even cruel, accusations. People will call me strange things and think of me in ways that do not reflect who I really am — this goes with the territory on which I stand.

I stand for the fundamentals of the faith. However, I am not necessarily going to stand behind all that has been identified as 'fundamentalism'. For instance, I do not expect, much less demand, that society as a whole adopt social and political agendas of my own. I have accepted that I live in a pluralistic society, which is essentially post-Christian. By this, I mean that Christianity is rapidly becoming a minority faith, and our society is not governed by a biblical ethic. I must recognize this or I will be forever disappointed, discouraged and angry. In addition, I am satisfied with people forming their own conclusions about how they will live their lives. Even when I see actions that I think are less than biblical, I will not react with judgements against people who are not interested in adhering to the biblical standard. But I know, and hope to some degree, that the believer, at any rate, will grow up to the fulness of Jesus as God works his will and ways into their lives. Living in the midst of this fallen world, I know I am *in* it but not *of* it. I am careful to keep my 'light' out in the open and burning as brightly as possible — I am not going to slink away with my tail between my legs.

Furthermore, I am careful to fight the right battles. Even some so-called important issues I will let go because they are not central to the core gospel of Christ.

In the right circumstances I will present a history of fundamentalism to people of good will who have a genuine interest in the subject. I will not 'cast pearls before swine', yet I have found many people appreciate coming to an understanding of the history of fundamental, as well as evangelical and reformed Christianity. Mainly, I am concerned that people do not close themselves off from Jesus for fear of being branded a fundamentalist. How sad that an unfounded fear, augmented with historical ignorance, should result in a person being cut off from God's love and salvation.

What labels fit me? I prefer simply 'Christian'. But I will accept evangelical, Protestant in the Reformed tradition, conservative, and even fundamentalist if I can set the historical context. I am a Christian because God the Father opened my eyes, my ears and my heart to hear Jesus' voice calling out to me. He saved me. He washed all my sin away. He gave me the gift of eternal life. His Spirit indwells me. I belong to him. He made me a part of his family, the church, both in heaven and on earth. This is who I am. Hang whatever other label you want to on me. I know who I am.

13.
What can the
unconverted do?

13.
What can the unconverted do?

A change in theology

After twenty-nine years of ministry with an Arminian viewpoint I underwent a theological transformation. Much of the change was the result of studying the first and second Great Awakenings in America. I am now 'reforming' and it has been quite a jolt to the church I pastor. A number have left the church, some have been converted, and yet others have come to the conclusion they are unconverted, but they remain in the church fellowship. What these precious seekers can do to become converted is a critical issue for me right now.

What can they do?

I used to have an easy answer to this question. 'Pray this sinner's prayer,' was my usual response. Now I know that the result will probably be a false conversion, or, as I like to say, 'christianization', rather than genuine conversion. But can I have any response at all and still be true to the Reformed tradition, which I believe more closely adheres to the biblical model? I believe so.

The unconverted may seek God, his kingdom and his righteousness.

The problems

Two problems must be addressed. First, the unconverted are dead in trespasses and sins (Ephesians 2:1) and thus have no will to do anything but continue in rebellion against God. Second, 'The god of this age has blinded the minds of unbelievers, so that they cannot see the light of the gospel of the glory of Christ, who is the image of God' (2 Corinthians 4:4). Between sin and Satan, the unconverted are in a desperate condition.

How can the problems be overcome? The Holy Spirit is the answer. When the gospel is preached the Holy Spirit will convict of sin, reveal Jesus and draw the unconverted to the cross. This is clear from John's Gospel chapters 14, 15 and 16. In a way in which we do not fully understand, by the working of God's Spirit, the unconverted are given the will and ability to come to Jesus. In fact, there is great responsibility laid upon the unconverted to trust in Jesus; they must repent of sin and believe in Jesus as Saviour and Lord.

The call to preach

To those unconverted at my own and other churches the Word of God says, 'Blessed are they who keep his statutes and seek him with all their heart.' 'I love those who love me, and those who seek me find me.' 'Seek the LORD while he may be found; call on him while he is near.' 'But seek first his kingdom and his righteousness, and all these things will be given to you as well.' 'Ask and it will be given to you; seek and you will find; knock and the door will be opened to you.' 'And without faith it is impossible to please God, because anyone who comes to him must believe that he exists and that he rewards those who earnestly seek him' (Psalm 119:2; Proverbs 8:17; Isaiah 55:6; Matthew 6:33; 7:7; and Hebrews 11:6).

As the gospel is preached the miraculous drawing occurs. There is often a great hunger for forgiveness and a desire to be right with God. There may be a great dread of hell and a desire to be safe in Christ. This is the work of the Holy Spirit and a work we should expect when the gospel is preached. As Paul explained, 'Faith comes from hearing the message, and the message is heard through the word of Christ' (Romans 10:17).

Cornelius' prayer

When Cornelius, the Roman centurion, sought after the God of Israel, the angel of the Lord said to him: 'Your prayers and gifts to the poor have come up as a memorial offering before God' (Acts 10:4). Though he was yet unconverted, God heard his prayers. Based on this, I urge unconverted people who are seeking Jesus to pray for two things. Firstly, pray that they would see their sin as it truly is; and secondly, pray that Jesus and his finished work might be clear to them. When a person wishes to pray such prayers, then that to me is evidence of the working of the Holy Spirit.

The Seeker and the seeker

God is the seeker of those who seek him; it is God alone who initiates the process. He is the great and good Shepherd who seeks for the wandering sheep; he is the one who diligently sweeps the house until the lost coin is found. And, he will find those he is seeking.

14.
'I don't care any more!'

14.
'*I don't care any more!*'

'How did it happen, Francisco, that you gave up?' I asked. 'I just don't care any more. What difference does it make anyway? As hard as I try, I keep ending up back here in prison.'

A familiar theme

Though I may hear this from a John Smith, a Hector Lopez, a Tyrone Jackson, or a Jack Ten Eagles on my visits to San Quentin Prison, it is the cry of despair and resignation. Emanating often from a giant reservoir of anger, directed towards both society and self, it is an attitude that surely condemns a person to a life of pain.

I am acquainted with it myself. After my divorce in which I lost everything — my family, my job, my home, even my car — I felt as if I didn't care what happened to me any more. It was as if I had entered a black hole. For two solid years I walked around depressed and behaved as though it didn't matter if I lived or died. I am convinced that if the God of the twenty-third Psalm had not walked with me during that time I would have in fact died, if not literally, then in every other way. But even during the darkest days I knew I belonged to Jesus and that he belonged to me. In a way I do not understand, he lifted me up out of the 'slimy pit, out of the mud and mire', and set my feet, once again, on the solid rock. So, at the prison, I feel as though I am indeed a beggar telling another beggar that there is hope.

How does it happen?

Sin is mysterious and it is powerful, and it is something that is in us all. Sin separates us from God: we know this, and it separates us from others, even ourselves. We all end up alone; even in a loving family we are alone, that is, deep inside us. If we follow our rebellious nature and are not reigned in or rescued by circumstances — family, friends, the law, the school, the church, and so on — the sin will work like a cancer in us, destroying us a little bit at a time. After a while, all can be lost, every dream dashed to pieces, and we don't care any more. Into the dark cloud we go, and our blindness overwhelms us.

Of course, this does not happen to us all like it did to Francisco, or even to me; most of us do not get to the very bottom. But we may all approach it. Some days simply go wrong. Bad day may be added to bad week and then joined to awful months. It may be illness, financial disaster, extreme family troubles, rejections, losses, major discouragements — with little light at the end of the tunnel. And if there is no strong foundation like there was for me, well, anything might happen.

Never give up!

Forgiveness of sin is a wonderful thing. Knowing that God is real and that he cares for us is most powerful. The fact that this world is not our ultimate home brings us great hope and joy. Jesus went to the very end of all things for us, dying in our place. He took the worst there is and did it for us. However bad it gets, Jesus can rescue us. He does it all the time, too. To the Franciscos, and the rest, I can confidently assure them that though they have given up on themselves, Jesus has not. He is like that Father who sees his runaway son coming back home and hurries to embrace him; or like the Good Shepherd who walks the dreaded places searching for lost and wounded sheep. He never gives up, so even if you don't care any more, you must never give up either.

15.
How it works

15.
How it works

This title is taken from the 'big book' of Alcoholics Anonymous, chapter 5, which is sometimes read at their meetings. It explains the basics of the famous '12 Step Program', and because of its simplicity and clarity, it is helpful to new members in particular. Similarly this chapter intends to express, with some simplicity and hopefully some clarity, how the Christian life works.

It is a mystery

How the Christian life works is a mystery. This admission may seem to compromise the goal of simplicity and clarity, even bring it into question altogether, but it must be stated since it is the truth. How a person, from a human perspective, becomes a Christian in the first place is not easily explained and it is not completely understood by anyone. The Bible is not laid out in a doctrinally systematic format; rather, we find small portions of hundreds of doctrinal points scattered throughout. But when the key points on salvation are put together, it becomes plain that conversion, the new birth, becoming a Christian, being saved (all synonymous terms) describe a work that God actually does, spiritually, within, for, and to a person.

That salvation is the one great concern is the testimony of both Scripture and Christian doctrine regardless of denomination. Separated as we are from God due to sin, only judgement and eternal death await the unconverted. This is the greatest of losses and God in his love reaches out to us in Christ.

The outline

The outline of this chapter is comprised of two points: salvation and sanctification. It is necessary to use such words; we must not be afraid of them, for they contain the essence of how it works.

Salvation means conversion, or how it is that a person is saved or born again. It encompasses repentance and faith. Sanctification describes the spiritual growing up or maturation of a Christian. This is analogous to the physical birth of a human being and the natural process of growing into maturity. To put it in the form of an equation: salvation or spiritual birth=physical birth, and sanctification=growing up.

1. Salvation

Before anyone is ever converted, he will hear the basic tenets of the gospel of Jesus Christ, which involves the crucifixion, death, burial and resurrection of Jesus,

Messiah and Lord. The gospel message may be communicated through a book, a film, or a personal conversation, but it is usually communicated through preaching. This is clearly depicted in Romans 10:17: 'So faith comes from what is heard, and what is heard comes by the preaching of Christ' (RSV).

Faith is a gift from God. 'For it is by grace you have been saved, through faith — and this not from yourselves, it is the gift of God — not by works, so that no one can boast' (Ephesians 2:8-9). No one has faith apart from it being given by the Holy Spirit. This much is clear. No one can repent unless sin is seen for what it is and it is the Holy Spirit who reveals this truth. No one has the capacity to repent and believe therefore without the influence of God. This is what is meant by grace — God makes it possible to repent and believe since no one can do it alone.

It is God's Holy Spirit who reveals to a person that he has sinned against God, who produces a desire to turn from that sin, and then reveals Jesus to be the Saviour who is able and willing to forgive all sin. Then the great mystery of conversion occurs. In a way we do not fully understand, a person is 'born again'. Salvation is completely a work of God. It does not result from a person's good deeds.

Someone might ask at this juncture: 'What can I do?' A jailer in the ancient city of Philippi asked this very question of the apostle Paul. The response: 'Believe in the Lord Jesus' (Acts 16:31). The jailer believed right there and then. How did he do it? Well, we are not told exactly how, except that it was by the power of God.

So, then, how can you believe in Jesus? You will only believe by the influence of God's Holy Spirit, which begins with the Spirit of God creating in you the desire to believe in Jesus, just as he did with the Philippian jailer. To go beyond this is to go beyond Scripture itself. The invitation is to repent of your sin and believe in Jesus. Anyone can do this since the Bible says that whosoever will may come to him. I will add: 'Look to Jesus and be saved.'

2. Sanctification

Sanctification means to be set aside by God as his own and for his service, and it begins right at the moment of conversion. In fact, each Christian is thoroughly sanctified or made holy by God at the instant of his conversion. This is why Christians are called 'saints', a term derived from the word 'sanctified'. A Christian is a saint and is holy, or sanctified, not because of anything the Christian has done, but solely because of what God has done. God has placed both within every Christian the righteousness of Jesus, and the Christian into Jesus, who is holy and without any blemish or sin. This is not an easy concept to grasp, but it is thoroughly biblical.

Although the Christian is sanctified, is considered completely holy by God, he still continues to sin. This is indeed paradoxical, but again, it is what the Scripture teaches. This has been the experience of Christians right from the beginning. We have been born anew by the Spirit of God, we have been given the gift of eternal life, yet we find ourselves sinning.

Not that the Christian is to continue in sin as a way of life. No, we are to turn away from sin and seek to honour and please God. But there is within us the mystery of sin, something incredibly powerful, that will sometimes gain certain victories over us. Nevertheless, despite our sin, the sureness of our salvation is never in question. Our salvation depends on what God has done in Christ and not upon our ability or strength to refrain from sinning.

Sanctification is a process that continues throughout our lifetime. We go forward little by little; sometimes we even seem to be going backwards. Paul put it this way: 'continue to work out your salvation with fear and trembling, for it is God who works in you to will and to act according to his good purpose' (Philippians 2:12-13). Paul urges the Christian to 'work out your salvation' while at the same time asserting that God is at work in the life of the Christian to do that very thing. It is a paradox. We cling to both of these truths simultaneously.

Assurance and peace

In reality it works as we trust in Jesus. This is it in a nutshell; but everything is centred on the fact that Jesus has secured our salvation and sanctification.

Jesus is the source of our assurance and peace. We have eternal life right now, and God is continually working with us, bringing us to maturity in Christ.

16.
How we know we are Christians

16.

How we know we are Christians

'Am I a Christian?' Since no certificate of authentication comes to us from the hand of God upon conversion, the answer to this critical question must ultimately be an experience of faith.

It is one thing to 'claim' salvation, as though one could, but it is quite another to know one has been 'claimed'. However, we can have clear indications that we are. It is much like the evidence that exists to prove we are human beings. Humans look like, act like, and think like human beings. Jesus' characterization of conversion as a spiritual new birth was neither random nor careless; it was a deliberate analogy. As there are traits associated with humanness, so too there are traits associated with being a born-again Christian. And it is on the basis of the presence of spiritual traits that we can 'know by faith' that we are indeed Christians.

This chapter is divided into two sections. The first section concerns those experiences that normally come *before* conversion, and the second section outlines those experiences that *normally*, but not always, come *after* conversion. These are set in a particular order in terms of spiritual experiences, but this should not be relied upon.

Experiences do, of course, differ to some degree. In addition, one should not be too particular in matching his or her experience with those given here. Since each person is different, considerable variation can be expected in how the Holy Spirit works. However, there is a common core of spiritual experiences that come to most people.

The following points have either been experienced by myself, someone I know, or someone I have read about.

Before conversion

- There may be a sense of meaninglessness or purpose-lessness. Some have described it as a spiritual or emotional restlessness. It may be intense and last for a long period of time. Or, it may be mild and of short duration, but all the while life seems somewhat disjointed and uneasy.
- A desire that the grave is not the end of life. Some have had a sense of anger that life could be so short and harsh. 'There must be more than this' expresses the hope for life after death. This is not so much a fear of death as it is a love of life.
- A sense that there will be a judgement. This was my experience and I could not account for it.
- A sense of being lost and alone, abandoned and orphaned. This most unpleasant feeling troubles us persistently and will not let us go.
- There may be anger and confusion, even anxiety, at being so vulnerable and out of control. Friends might

suggest therapy at such a time, but if the advice is
followed, it provides no real relief.

- A sense of unworthiness, of having done wrong, of
feeling guilty, even of being ashamed may descend
upon us. This sense of ourselves persists even though
we affirm philosophies that are relativistic and that
have no moral content.

- A sharp, even painful realization of having broken
God's holy laws and thus standing condemned before
him. This is a major step beyond the previous experience. Here there is a clear and unmistakable recog-
nition that God is real and that we are lawbreakers.

- A sense of being spiritually naked, wretched and mis-
erable. This, again, is a step beyond the previous experience and is most uncomfortable. It is somewhat
rare in the conversion experiences I have read but
not absent completely, as the testimonies of George
Whitefield and John Bunyan reveal.

- There may be a period of trying to be self-righteous.
We attempt to strike a balance between sins and good
actions. Performing good deeds produce a temporary
sense of well-being, which is followed by failures that
produce a sense of personal disgust.

- The goal is to be a 'good person'. There may be a
sensitivity, almost of a paranoid nature, that others,
particularly Christians, are judging us and thinking
we are not good people.

- Attempts at severe religiosity, even involving material self-denial, may be seriously engaged in. This is
rare but not unheard of.

- Giving up on the attempt to become acceptable to
God. Some resign themselves to a hopeless condition

and fear they will never be good enough to receive forgiveness.

- A sense, sometimes accompanied with an inner desperation, of having a hardened heart and a callous mind. Some may even feel out of touch with reality.
- Efforts may be made to understand the Bible and actually get to the bottom of what Christianity is all about.
- An interest in Jesus begins to take form. Out of fear of being ridiculed, we keep this interest a secret. Some, however, are aggressive in their seeking and don't care who knows or thinks what.
- In some manner or other, we are exposed to the gospel. It may be via preaching, a personal conversation, a book or other printed material, a song, even a conversation overheard at a coffee shop. Here the biblical pattern is verified: 'So faith comes from what is heard, and what is heard comes by the preaching of Christ' (Romans 10:17, RSV).
- Now, the Holy Spirit is drawing or calling us to Christ. Little else matters now. Only two things are clear: our own sinfulness and the forgiveness that is in Jesus.
- It is as though Jesus himself is calling out to us.
- It is as though we hear his voice and nothing can keep us from him.
- Jesus is now irresistible and calls us to himself.
- Conversion or the new birth occurs. We do not know how or what or why, but there is a newness. It may happen quietly or with great emotion or something in-between.

After conversion

- Some are immediately joyful and have a sense of being at rest.
- Some feel as though a great burden has lifted from their shoulders.
- Some feel nothing at all.
- Some, like I was, are confused initially. Yet the inner spiritual conflict has ended.
- Some are fearful as to what the change in them will bring. I was worried that I would lose friends. My mother's reaction was a major concern, as I knew she was antagonistic towards Christianity.
- Some will experience rejection from family and friends.
- Some will have a great desire, which is very unusual for them, to read the Bible. This was certainly true of me, as I could not find enough time to read it.
- Some will want to be with other Christians, even attend church and worship. At first the newness and strangeness associated with worship and hymn-singing may be uncomfortable, but the 'baby' Christian knows where he will be nurtured.
- Some will be drawn to prayer and will spend long periods praying to God. The sudden realization that God is real, that he loves and cares for us, that there is an actual reason for existence is quite overwhelming and we love to fellowship with God.
- Some will, and usually fearfully, attempt to tell others what happened to them.
- Some will decide to keep it all a secret, especially after they are rebuffed by significant people in their lives due to their testimony.

- Some will want to join a Bible study to learn all they possibly can about Jesus and the Bible. Though everything that is said and taught is not quickly understood, there will be a persistence in 'growing in the Word'.
- There may be an initial period of euphoria, but this will end and things will seem, emotionally speaking, much as it was before the conversion.
- Sin may become an issue. Some will have the sense that they are hopeless sinners, some will be mad that so much of their life was sin-oriented, and some will think they are not good enough to be a Christian. This last one was true of me. Not understanding that sanctification was a lifelong process and that I had already been declared righteous in Christ, I seriously thought about dropping out altogether.
- Some will end one sin only to find another one to deal with, or even a new sin will come along. Occasionally a new Christian will feel hopeless, only to discover that indeed they are not righteous at all and that only Jesus is.
- There is a continuing desire to turn away from sin.
- Identifying with Jesus and other Christians, even when it means censor or rejection from others, comes to characterize us. For me this meant ostracism from some friends and co-workers.
- There is a desire for water baptism.
- There is a desire to receive the Lord's Supper.
- There is a desire to be of service and to be faithful with material possessions. I experienced this about six months after my conversion. At first I sang in the choir and put just a minimal amount in the offering

plate. Before long I was teaching a junior high Sunday school class and tithing my money.

- A desire to please and honour God. This becomes a continuing desire and lifelong expression of our love for God.
- A continuing sense of our own unworthiness.
- A continuing dependency on Jesus and his righteousness.
- A delight in hearing the gospel preached; hearing a good sermon becomes more important than going to a sporting or musical event.
- Sunday becomes a special day for worship, ministry and rest.
- We feel constrained to give up a 'habit' because we come to believe it is not pleasing to God.
- Being faithful with money even when funds are running short.
- Appreciation for and love of hymn lyrics such as:
  'Amazing grace! how sweet the sound, that saved a wretch like me!'
  'There is a fountain filled with blood'
  'My Jesus, I love Thee'
  'For Thee all the follies of sin I resign'
  'Tell me the story of Jesus, Write on my heart every word'
  'Fairest Lord Jesus! Thee will I honour, Thou, my soul's Glory, Joy, and Crown!'
  'O for a thousand tongues to sing my great Redeemer's praise.'
  'Jesus, the very thought of Thee with sweetness fills my breast.'

'My richest gain I count but loss, and pour contempt on all my pride.'
'So I'll cherish the old rugged cross.'
'Would He devote that sacred head for such a worm as I?'

It would have been impossible for me to sing words such as these before my conversion; and, it took a while to get used to them, but once I did, I loved them.

- A determination to follow Jesus despite doubts. A settled and fixed theology does not come with conversion. Early on I thought everything I heard from the pulpit and from my new Christian friends was absolute truth. Later, I had to make each and every point of doctrine my own. This is not easily or quickly done.
- If a major failure occurs, even a moral scandal, the person of faith will still, eventually, continue to trust in Jesus. I have had my problems but by God's grace he did not abandon me or correct me so harshly that I gave up on myself.
- Even in the midst of mental, theological and emotional confusion there is a determination to love and follow Jesus though we should be cast into hell. I noticed that some of the English and American Puritans spoke like this and it took me some time to understand that they were expressing their fallibility while upholding God's sovereignty.
- A desire that our life should glorify God.
- A desire that our death should glorify God.
- A desire that at the judgement of Christ we would hear him say to us, 'Well done, good and faithful servant, enter into the joy of your rest.'

A wide range of excellent books on spiritual subjects is available from Evangelical Press. Please write to us for your free catalogue or contact us by e-mail.

Evangelical Press
Faverdale North Industrial Estate, Darlington, DL3 0PH, England

Evangelical Press USA
P. O. Box 84, Auburn, MA 01501, USA

e-mail: sales@evangelicalpress.org

web: www.evangelicalpress.org